TEN LECTURES ON
PSYCHOTHERAPY AND
SPIRITUALITY

TEN LECTURES ON PSYCHOTHERAPY AND SPIRITUALITY

Editor

Nathan Field

With the assistance of Trudy Harvey and Belinda Sharp

KARNAC

LONDON   NEW YORK

First published in 2005 by
H. Karnac (Books) Ltd.
6 Pembroke Buildings, London NW10 6RE

British Library Cataloguing in Publication Data

A C.I.P. for this book is available from the British Library

ISBN 1 85575 352 9

Edited, designed and produced by The Studio Publishing Services Ltd,
Exeter EX4 8JN

Printed in Great Britain by Hobbs the Printers Ltd

10 9 8 7 6 5 4 3 2 1

www.karnacbooks.com

CONTENTS

ACKNOWLEDGEMENTS

Grateful thanks are due to Vernon Yorke for giving generously of his time in making tape transcripts of all contributions in the original lecture series; and to Lucy Wilkinson in transcribing many of them into text.

ABOUT THE CONTRIBUTORS

Karen Armstrong entered an English teaching order of nuns in 1962 , taking her vows three years later. In 1967 her order sent her to Oxford to read English. She completed her degree in 1970, having left her order the previous year. From 1973 to 1976 she held the post of tutorial research fellow at Bedford College and taught literature at London University. She is currently teaching at Leo Baeck College for the study of Judaism and the training of Rabbis. She is one of the world's foremost religious commentators, with a number of acclaimed books to her name, the most recent being *The Struggle for God*.

Bernardine Bishop has a background in academic English, writing and teaching. She is a psychoanalytic psychotherapist in private practice in London, and a Full Member of the London Centre for Psychotherapy and the Lincoln Centre.

David M. Black is a psychoanalyst and founding Member of the Foundation for Psychotherapy and Counselling. He has published a number of papers on psychoanalysis and its relation to science and the religions.

Ronald Britton initially studied medicine at University College London. He worked in both adult and child psychiatry before committing himself to psychoanalytic practice. During the 1970s he was chairman of the Department for Children and Parents at the Tavistock Clinic, where his special interest was in the provision of psychotherapy for severely deprived and abused children. He is a psychoanalyst in private practice and a training and supervising analyst of the British Psychoanalytic Society. His most recent publication is *Sex, Death and the Superego* (Karnac, 2003).

Patrick Casement was originally a social worker before training with the British Association of Psychotherapists. He is a training and supervising analyst of the British Psychoanalytic Society, and a psychoanalyst in private practice. His publications include *On Learning from the Patient* and *Learning from our Mistakes: Beyond Dogma in Psychoanalysis and Psychotherapy*.

Adrian Dickinson is a Full Member of the London Centre for Psychotherapy, having qualified in 1990, and has a private practice in London. He taught English Literature at various Independent Schools for twenty-eight years and has given talks and conducted seminars on his particular interest: the English Romantic poets as precursors of psychoanalytic thinking, for the LCP, the C. G. Jung Analytical Psychology Club, and the Forum for Independent Psychotherapists.

Nathan Field trained as a Jungian analyst with the British Association of Psychotherapists in the 1960s and has now retired from private practice. Formerly Chair and Fellow of the London Centre for Psychotherapy, he is the author of *Breakdown and Breakthrough: Psychotherapy in a New Dimension*, and recently founded the Scribble Society.

Rosemary Gordon gained her PhD in psychology at the University of London and later worked as a senior clinical psychologist at Napsbury Hospital. She is a professional member and training analyst of the Society of Analytical Psychology, a Fellow of the Royal Anthropological Institute and of the British Psychological Society. Her books include *Bridges: Metaphor for Psychic Processes*.

Josephine Klein was originally a university teacher of theories of social life before training as a psychotherapist. She is a Fellow of the London Centre for Psychotherapy and a member of the British Association of Psychotherapists. Her books include *Doubts and Certainties in the Practice of Psychotherapy*, and *Jacob's Ladder: Essays on Experiences of the Ineffable in the Context of Contemporary Psychotherapy* (2003).

Tom McDonnell received degrees in both Law and Arts from Melbourne University. During his time as an undergraduate he also commenced vocal studies at the Melba Conservatorium. In 1966 he came to England to begin an international career as an opera and concert singer. He has sung frequently at Covent Garden, the English National Opera, and at many major opera houses throughout the world. Between 1984 and 1994 he worked with the Opera Factory London/Zurich, a group ensemble dedicated to innovative approaches to contemporary and classical opera. In 1990, while still involved in opera, he began training at the London Centre for Psychotherapy, qualifying in 1996. He is now a member of the LCP Council, the Professional Practice Committee, and is in full time private practice.

Chris MacKenna is an Anglican clergyman, a Full Member of the Jungian Analytic Section of the British Association of Psychotherapists, and currently Director of the Saint Marylebone Healing and Counselling Centre. Publications include " Jung and Christianity--wrestling with God" which appeared in *Jungian Thought in the Modern World*.

David Mayers studied and taught philosophy, specializing in the work of Wittgenstein, before training in psychoanalytic psychotherapy when he became greatly influenced by Donald Meltzer's work. He is now in private practice and teaches extensively in clinical and academic settings. He is currently working on the mutual influences of Beckett and Bion.

Steven Mendoza is a member of the London Centre for Psychotherapy, where he was a teacher for some years. His education was initially in biology. After a sojourn as a film editor's assistant, he took a degree in psychology and worked as a social worker as a pre-liminary to training as a psychotherapist. He was briefly a student of the Dharma of Sakyamuni Buddha and has a particular interest in what Buddhism and psychoanalysis share. His paper "The emerging religious dimension of knowing in psychoanalysis" is published by Karnac in *Elusive Elements in Practice* in the Practice of Psychotherapy Series.

Donald Meltzer (1923–2004) trained in medicine and child psychi-atry in the United States. He came to London in 1954 and had his training analysis with Melanie Klein until her death in 1960. For many years a leading member of the Kleinian group, he was instru-mental in developing a Kleinian child psychotherapy training. He is the author of many influential psychoanalytic books.

Andrew Samuels is Professor of Analytical Psychology at the University of Essex, Visiting Professor in Psychoanalytic Studies at Goldsmith's College, University of London, and a training analyst of the Society of Analytical Psychology. He is also the Co-founder of Psychotherapists and Counsellors for Social Responsibility and of Antidote, the campaign for emotional literacy, and a Trustee, Work–Life Balance Trust. Publications, which have been translated into nineteen languages, include *Jung and the Post-Jungians* (1985), *The Father* (1985), *A Critical Dictionary of Jungian Analysis* (1986), *The Plural Psyche* (1989), *Psychopathology* (1989), *The Political Psyche* (1993), and *Politics on the Couch: Citizenship and the Internal Life* (2001).

Jennifer Silverstone is a member of the London Centre for Psychotherapy. She is in full time private practice and is a training therapist and supervisor. Her most recent paper 'An absence of mind', which appeared in *Ideas in Practice*, explores the theme that where there is an absence of internal space in the mother's mind, her baby can become fearful of thought.

Hester Solomon is a training analyst and supervisor for the Jungian Section of the British Association of Psychotherapists. She is past Chair of the BAP's Jungian Training, of the BAP's Council, and of the BAP's Ethics Committee. She is currently Vice-President of the

International Association for Analytical Psychology. She lectures widely in the UK and abroad and is author of numerous articles on analytical psychology and psychoanalysis. She has co-edited *Jungian Thought in the Modern World, Contemporary Jungian Clinical Practice,* and *The Ethical Attitude in Analytic Practice.*

Kenneth Wright is a psychiatrist, psychoanalyst, and psychotherapist. He trained with the Independent Group of the British Psychoanalytic Society and at the Tavistock Clinic. He lectures nationally and internationally and has written numerous papers on creativity. He is the author of *Vision and Separation: Between Mother and Baby,* which was awarded the Margaret Mahler Prize in 1992. He lives in Suffolk and works in private practice.

INTRODUCTION

The lectures that comprise this book were delivered at monthly intervals in 2002 at the London Centre for Psychotherapy. Within a few weeks of their announcement nearly every seat was sold for the whole year. No doubt the audience were attracted by the reputation of the speakers on the programme; but even more interesting was the degree of interest that the linking of psychotherapy and spirituality aroused in the counselling and psychotherapy community.

When Freud discovered (or invented) psychoanalysis just over a century ago, any association with the notion of spirituality was virtually unthinkable. Some years earlier, on taking up his position as a researcher in neuroscience at the Helmholtz Institute of Vienna, Freud had been required to "swear an oath to be true to the tenets of Science" (see Gordon, this volume). It must be remembered that Science and Religion had been enemies since the seventeenth century. In his paper, David Black describes how Galileo, whom he calls "the originator of the scientific mind", was threatened with torture, and possibly death, by the Inquisition for his heretical ideas. In spite of humbly disavowing his epoch-making ideas and discoveries, they still cost him his liberty, and almost his life.

But, over the next three centuries, Science decisively prevailed. Freud, as a dedicated scientist and determined to protect his fledgeling psychoanalysis from the criticism that it did not qualify as a science, aimed to base his theories on firm biological foundations. Religion he regarded as a collective obsessional neurosis, God he reduced to an idealized projection of the father, and spirituality, in the form of mystical experience such as the "oceanic" feeling, he understood to be "the restoration of limitless narcissism". This reductionist view prevailed amongst Freud's disciples throughout most of the twentieth century. A characteristic example was Franz Alexander's brilliant paper entitled "Buddistic training as an artificial catatonia" (1931), by which he implied that intensive meditation induced neo-psychotic states of mind.

But from within the psychoanalytic movement itself there had been, from early on, dissenting voices which questioned Freud's insistence on the primacy of the sexual drive. Alfred Adler tried to replace the sex drive with the drive to power. Adler's attempt failed: he fell into Freud's disfavour, defected from the psychoanalytic movement, and is now rarely mentioned.

The most serious challenge to Freud's reductionist approach came from Jung, originally groomed as Freud's successor. While accepting that dysfunctions of the personality are massively affected by childhood experience, Jung insisted that not everything that forms the personality can be attributed to the past. Confronted by symptoms we need to ask not only: "What caused this?" but also "What can this be *for*?" Jung's search for both causes and meanings led him to explore the spiritual potential in human nature and its possible link with psychopathology. Thus he could declare: "The gods have become diseases". Such a pronouncement carries the intriguing implication that some sorts of mental illness may harbour the seeds of growth and creativity.

Freud himself, always an acute observer, could not help but note that "It is a very remarkable thing that the Ucs of one human being can react upon that of another, without passing through the Cs". And, in another paper, that "the scales weigh in favour of thought-transference". Yet, not much later he beseeched Jung to resist sinking into "the black tide of the occult". But it was already too late. The conceptual rift which opened up between these two very gifted men, who had once been deeply involved with each other, was one major cause that led to Jung's excommunication from mainstream psycho-analysis. Jung went on to develop his own approach, which he called analytical psychology. This has its distinctive theory and practice, but incorporates, particularly here in England, substantial amounts of psychoanalytic thinking and terminology. This is a tribute, as Hester Solomon points out in her response to Ron Britton, that psychoanalysis has largely neglected to return. In spite of spasmodic attempts to initiate a dialogue between Freudians, Kleinians, and Jungians, the original rift has more or less persisted to the present day.

With Jung's departure, psychoanalysis continued to evolve. In the UK, thanks to Fairbairn's critique of Freudian drive theory, the pioneering studies of Melanie Klein and Winnicott into infancy, Bowlby's researches into early attachment, and Balint's into the therapeutic aspects of regression, psychoanalysis was obliged to accommodate object relations theory. This, in turn, led to the redis-covery, by a different route and using a different terminology, a number of crucial concepts that Jung had arrived at earlier, most particularly the notion of a self as distinct from the ego. With grow-ing understanding of the counter-transference and borderline states, contemporary psychoanalysis has been obliged to acknowl-edge the puzzling manifestations of intersubjectivity, or what Josephine Klein calls in her paper the "intersect". More recently, thanks to the late work of the most radical of the post-Kleinian ana-lysts, W. R. Bion, psychoanalysts are presented with the prospect that, by following the true path of psychoanalysis, they will come closer to the mystical knowledge of God.

During the same historical period the physicists were exploring the structure of the universe and the atom. To make sense of their discoveries, Einstein formulated Relativity and the four dimen-sional space-time continuum; Heisenberg arrived at the Uncer-tainty Principle; Bohm proposed that the material universe is the "explicate" manifestion of some immaterial "implicate order". All the old scientific certainties of materialism, determinism, reduc-tionism, causality, and objectivity, to which Freud had sworn alle-giance, began to dissolve. As Rosemary Gordon's paper describes, the time-honoured boundaries between mind and matter became ever more elusive and paradoxical.

The foregoing developments, now widely discussed in the psy-choanalytic literature, influenced my approach in organizing these lectures. If, within the bastions of "hard" science, inner experience has become a legitimate topic of discussion; if even the major figures in the world of physics—Einstein, Heisenberg, Pauli, and Bohm—could publicly acknowledge a spiritual perspective, perhaps the time was ripe to attempt a modest resumption of the aborted collaboration between Freud and Jung?

With the cooperation of Belinda Sharp, then chair of the LCP Professional Activities Section, I invited a more or less equal number of prominent psychoanalysts and analytical psychologists to offer their thoughts on the links between psychotherapy and spirituality.

To facilitate the possibility of a Jungian-Freudian dialogue, I tried, but did not always succeed, in matching each lecturer with a respondent from the other side. Moreover, the respondents' task was much trickier than I had imagined: they were expected to show an informed appreciation of the lecturer's contribution, but to present a dynamic challenge to their leading ideas. Inevitably, some pairings have proved more dynamic than others, and two of the respondents declined to appear in print.

My own task in this Introduction, which I felt required me to take an overview of the whole series, has also proved more difficult than I expected. The range of topics and approaches presented appear very diverse. Some contributions are theoretical, some historical, some personal. The majority of contributors find the links between psychotherapy and spirituality helpful and natural; others find them thoroughly incompatible. Some of these divergences rest on matters of definition: what is psychotherapy? And, far more problematic: what is spirituality? Does it really exist? And if so, does it belong in the consulting room?

There is a further divergence among those who do find it possible to reconcile psychotherapy and spirituality: one that seems to reflect the theological gulf between God and the Godhead; that is, between the deity who manifests his existence to mankind, and the One who is Unknowable. Among the former, Kenneth Wright found divinity in Nature, Donald Meltzer in the miracle of the child who can produce a 'well-formed stool', Jo Klein in the mystery of the 'intersect', and Andrew Samuels in a spectrum of human activities that ranges from social responsibility to joyous sex. Yet, in spite of all these divergences, I hope the reader shares with me the sense

that there is some ingredient, perhaps impossible to name, that
all these psychotherapy practitioners share. It seemed fitting to end
the book with a contribution from Karen Armstrong, who is not a
psychotherapist, but a distinguished historian of religion.

Nathan Field
Editor

The strange case of the missing spirit

Rosemary Gordon

"One makes a path by walking". This was written to me by James Roose-Evans on the fly-sheet of his book *Ritual Today*, and it seems to me helpful to all of us who seek to think, to reflect, and, with luck, to achieve some comprehension and, possibly, some experience, of spirit.

When I try to say what I mean by spirit the best definition that comes to mind is the word *Kwoth*; a term used by the Nuer—a simple Nilotic people in East Africa (Evans Pritchard, 1940). It is an onomatopoeic word, suggesting wind or breath. But it is what the Nuer say about *Kwoth* that I find so very impressive. They say of *Kwoth* that it is invisible and ubiquitous, like wind or air; it has no fixed abode, no material or sensuous quality, and therefore it cannot be experienced directly by the senses, and they say that therefore they do not know what *Kwoth* is "like". They say that they are "merely simple people" and cannot be expected to know about such matters, or to understand the mysteries of life and death. For spirit is such a mystery; it has no earthly form, is entirely indeterminate, and has no sanctuary. It cannot be thought of at all, and can only be contrasted with the material world that we know through the senses. What the Nuer say about *Kwoth* is quite astonishingly

1

close to how Michael Eigen has tried to describe Bion's "O" in his book *The Psychoanalytic Mystic:* "'O'" is inaccessible, yet nothing is more accessible, since 'O' is everywhere and everything. One cannot know 'O', but what else can one know?" (Eigen, 1998)

It was when I read about and studied some of the African religions that I discovered that all of them seem to have the same basic schema; a supreme being who lives in the sky, who has made the world, who is responsible for life and death, who is all-powerful, but is so far removed that he is not worshipped, nor has he a sanctuary, nor a specialized priesthood. But he sends out his sons or messengers, pieces of himself, and through these pieces, these little gods that are pieces of the Great God, he can communicate with us.

At first I thought that this cosmological schema was characteristic of African notions only. But when I looked at the writings of Mircea Eliade (1960) I found that in fact he recognized this schema to be world-wide. Is this not, in fact, the basic schema of Christianity: are we not familiar with it through the Christian beliefs in God and his son Jesus? Eliade observes that very often there could be the further complication that one of these sons, or messengers, or minor gods, becomes identified with, or mistaken for, the Great God, rather than being recognized as just a little god. It is the confusion of a piece of God with the Great God that tends to become the basis of the theistic religions. This has led to competition, rivalry, even wars between them, often between different followers of the same little god. Any one of these religions, or factions, is liable to claim that it has been granted a unique revelation, and that it alone has the one real and valid truth.

But there is also a positive side to this deintegrative process: the religious institutions, in their attempt to make spirit sensuous, perceptible, and, as it were, "embodied", have engaged in a great deal of art-making in and around their religious centres. This, in its turn, has led men and women to develop creativity, aesthetic sensitivity, and the capacity to somehow marry matter and spirit. Artwork, primarily in painting, sculpture, architecture, and music, seeks to express that which it is meant to serve. The very notion of God, the qualities and functions, dogmas, stories, images, metamorphoses, of a given religion are, in fact, attempts to make spirit more accessible to mankind; accessible, that is, to their more limited capacity to relate to, understand or to experience what is abstract; and above all what is ineffable.

The Nuer of Africa seem to have conceived religious concepts that are acutely sensitive, refined, and highly complex. This is in contrast to some of the "closed systems" adopted by many of the "higher religions", which have so often remained concretistic, opposed to change, to insight, and to experience from the inner world. Instead, the major world religions have facilitated splitting, projection, and differentiation into hostile camps, each being seduced by the illusion of certitude, omniscience, and narcissistic self-righteousness.

In other words Spirit, being essentially abstract and ineffable, deintegrates into smaller or simpler pieces of Itself. These then tend towards concretization and personification to form the major religious institutions, with their dogmas, ritual practices, and verbalizations. And together with the religions go their priesthoods and their works of art. Spirit is made nameable, conscious, even concrete, in a variety of ways: through ritualization, verbalization, music, architecture, and an elaborate priesthood.

The transformation of the spirit into religious institutions was required in order to meet some of mankind's basic psychological needs, such as the craving for certainty, the tangible, the nameable, the personal. Behind these needs lie deep human fears of pain, death, and oblivion. Humankind has the driving need to find some meaning in our brief passage from birth to death. As the Nuer express it so movingly, "We are simple people and cannot be expected to understand *Kwoth*, the Spirit, or life, or death." We too, each of us, in the face of the mystery of existence, are simple people. Yet we all find ourselves driven to confront, to search for, to listen for, to invent answers. We are all driven to do battle with the dread and joy our world offers us. We are all available to experience awe and wonderment, all potentially susceptible to the numinous, which signals the presence of "The Other", or "O"—a term coined by Bion, who has written about it in such an insightful way.

Bion, a much-bemedalled "hero" of the First World War, was in many respects a nineteenth-century man: yet he was also a charismatic analyst–psychiatrist, part-mystic, part-shaman. His notion of the "Other", or "O", is as indescribable a concept as that held by a Zen Master, or a Meister Eckhardt, or the Om of the Sanskrit mantra

Om mani padme hum, meaning "in the heart of the lotus is a jewel". Yet elusive or not, "O" formed the centre-piece of Bion's highly effective therapy, especially when accompanied by his silences, which could be agonizingly prolonged (Bion, 1970).

In a sense Bion *was* "O", and the half-mystical world that he inhabited was conceptually light-years away from that of Freud, who regarded mysticism in a strictly reductive way as the "restoration of limitless narcissism". Freud's view was characteristic of nineteenth-century science, which passed out in a final spasm of over-rational thought typified by the Helmholtz Institute of Vienna, whose staff, including the young Sigmund Freud, had to swear an oath to be true to the tenets of science. This science was bound by the iron rule that the observer remained the observer, and the observed remained the observed. Both observer and observed were separated by a conceptual and methodological chasm so deep as to be impassable.

This neat division was completely upset by the arrival of the quantum physics of Bohr and Heisenberg. In this new, sub-atomic microcosm, scientific truth ceased to be exact and was instead transmuted into an approximation. Helmholtz was confounded. It was the triumph of the new relativity where the observer *always* affected the observed. The only question was—to what degree? The new quantum-physical age would have been more familiar to the cavemen artists of the palaeolithic era than it was to the vast majority of nineteenth-century scientists. For the cavemen artists rocks and stones were as animate and connected a part of their world as the bison and mammoths that they drew and hunted, and the stone axes that they used.

One of the men who swam in this strange new quantum milieu was the brilliant mathematician and physicist, Wolfgang Pauli. It was Pauli who collaborated with Jung in the elaboration of the concept of synchronicity—the "acausal" connecting principle that clusters together "meaningful" events without overt causal links (Jung & Pauli, 1952). Pauli's physicist colleagues, only half in jest, attributed to him the power to stop their experiments in their tracks by his very presence. When he arrived on the premises, all machines, all experiments, mysteriously stopped working.

This new quantum-physical version of the caveman artist's animism ushered in the new age of indeterminacy and connectedness.

Everything was connected to everything else: the hunter to the hunted, the observer to the observed, life to death. The animated rocks, waterfalls, and wizards of our palaeolithic forebears seem to be in a direct line with Schroedinger's unfortunate—or was it fortunate?—cat, which, according to quantum theory, contrives to be both alive and dead at the same time. Some wheel, somewhere, seemed to have turned full-circle. Well before the mid-twentieth century it was once again politically correct for scientists to talk about "God" without being laughed off-stage by their colleagues.

One of the discoveries that had ushered in this paradigm shift was holography. It was brought into being by the Nobel Prize winner Denis Gabor, whose theoretical calculations had to await the birth of the laser before they could be verified by experiment. A hologram is, in essence, a special type of optical storage system that is best explained by example; if you take a holographic photograph of a horse, then the photographic plate that results seems to bear no image but that of a series of rather meaningless intersecting circles. If, however, you shine a laser beam through the holographic plate then, instantaneously, a fully three-dimensional vision of the horse emerges. You can even move round to "see" the back of the horse. Even stranger, if you snip off a corner of the hologram and illuminate that with the laser, then a slightly fuzzy but totally distinct three-dimensional image of the horse emerges. Incredibly, the part contains the whole—the whole of the whole! The hologram is a physical manifestation of the point I made earlier: that it is as a consequence of God disintegrating and breaking up into smaller pieces of Itself—into spirits or gods—that the religions evolve.

The Jungian analyst, Louis Zinkin, was captivated by the mystery of the hologram and wrote a lucid and most provocative paper entitled "The hologram as a model for analytical psychology". In his conclusions Louis Zinkin said:

> Jung wrote that one day it would be possible to integrate his psychology with physics, just as Freud hoped to integrate his psychology with biology. Perhaps this dream may never come true. The biggest obstacle is the sheer difficulty of understanding what the physicists are talking about. . . . they themselves are struggling to grasp all the implications of their own discoveries when these conflict with our existing view of the world . . . [Zinkin, 1987]

There is one written exchange that for me, above all, typifies the break in the log-jam in present thinking by the nuclear physicists. Let me say here that the physicists are, as usual, totally unafraid to voice their daring thoughts even if they bring down their own scientific edifices. The God that they follow is not that of Helmholtz but that of Carl Popper: they believe that progress, painful though it may be, comes through the falsification of hypotheses and the subsequent construction of a newer, more elegant hypothesis, rather than in clinging to the wreckage of the last one. Even the word God, as a sort of shorthand for some indescribable prime-mover, has reappeared in the vocabulary of the physicists, seemingly the most adventurous of the scientific thinkers. Compared to the apparent lunacies of this new quantum world, with its "many worlds theory", the concept of a creator God was relatively straight-forward.

Consider the following exchanges: in 1956 Wolfgang Pauli—a Nobel Prize winner for his discoveries in quantum physics—embarked on a long correspondence with his new friend, Aldous Huxley. Their letters, which centre on the relationship between science and mysticism, are embedded in the vast correspondence that Pauli conducted with his colleagues world-wide. Knowing of my interest, these unpublished letters were brought to my attention by Frank Steiner, professor of theoretical physics at Ulm University, where they are held.

I will begin with one from Pauli to Huxley:

> Dear Mr Huxley . . . Kepler is also a particular example within the frame of the more general problem of the relation between science and mystics which you have so often discussed in your essay. Just by his mystical qualities he was indeed driven into a new form of science and thereby into astronomical research. I do not know what after our passage from the age of natural sciences the future of mystics will be but I feel in a way similar to you that mystics contain possibilities of human experience which in some way should find its place and expression in any well-balanced culture. The particular problems of the relation between spirit and matter to which you allude also in your book *Heaven and Hell* are represented in my study of Kepler in the discussion of the controversy between Kepler and Robert Flood. I believe that the alchemy represented by the latter had some intuitive knowing of such connections between

matter and spirit which you had in mind, and that this knowing was getting lost in the age of natural science.

Huxley replies on 10 June 1956:

Thank you very much for your kind letter. This question of the relation between inner and outer reality is a very interesting one. The literal interpretation of the saying "as above so below" seems to lead those who accept it into all kinds of false analogies . . . I would say that the connection between the inner and the outer is on a level far deeper than that on which any kind of symbol can be perceived. The mystics talk of a state of "obscure knowledge" in which there is an immediate experience of ALL in ONE and ONE in ALL. Or the total presence of the absolute in every relative, of eternity and time, or Nirvana and Samsara. There is a kind of total omniscience but no clear knowledge of any particular aspect of the world. The obscure knowledge makes possible for those who have had it a more understanding attitude in relation to events, things and persons, but it does not cast any light on concrete problems in astronomy, biology, physics, and so forth. The fact that, in Kepler's case, a religious symbol contributed to the correct working of a scientific hypothesis seems to me to be in a sense accidental . . . the most wonderful thing about the mind is that it is more than the personal self, more than the collective unconscious stocked with archetypal images—it is also a series of "not-selves" culminating in the supreme non-self, the Atman, the Void, the suchness, which is at the same time the Self—the Self of every sentient being. The clearest recognition of this primordial fact is to be found amongst the exponents of Zen Buddhism who have no use for symbols, and aim at getting out of their own light in such a way that they may be filled with an obscure knowledge of the non-particular, that is in particular the "not-thought" that lies beyond thought—the Buddha-nature or Suchness that is present in every instance and in every event, every relationship, for those who can forget the nonsense of a world accepted at its face value along with the more solemn philosophico-religious nonsense of a world in which everything is a "gleichnis" for something else. Something which in spite of its sublimity remains all too human . . .

Pauli replied to this on the 10 August.

. . . But my real problem was, and is, the relationship between mysticism and science—what is different between them and what is common. I can assure you that for me, as a modern scientist, the difference is less obvious than it is for the layman. Both mystics and scientists have the same aim—to become aware of the unity of the knowledge of Man and the Universe and to forget our own small Ego. And what is a symbol for me? There are different levels of abstraction . . . we speak in mathematical symbols or models about the reality of physics. And yet expressions like "obscure knowledge", "ray of the Godhead" which you use, are they not symbols too?

I recently "chanced" upon a description of the part that intuition can play in scientific discovery. It concerns how Enrico Fermi found a way of turning "fast" neutrons into "slow" ones: a discovery that was to lead to the atomic bomb. Firmi's team were trying to find out whether a beam of neutrons could produce new isotopes, which it did. But their results were strangely inconsistent. In an attempt to track down the inconsistency Fermi devised a lead filter which he planned to insert into the neutron beam. Fermi's account of what happened next is a splendid example of what Huxley meant by "obscure knowledge":

> I will tell you how I came to make the discovery which I suppose is the most important one that I have ever made. One day, as I came to the laboratory, it occurred to me that I should examine the effect of placing a piece of lead before the incident neutrons. And instead of my usual custom, I took great pains to have the piece of lead precisely machined. I was clearly dissatisfied with something. I tried every excuse to postpone putting the piece of lead in its place. When finally with some reluctance I was going to put it into its place, I said to myself: "No, I do not want this piece of lead here, what I want is a piece of paraffin [wax]". It was just like that; with no advance warning, no prior reasoning. I immediately took some odd piece of paraffin [wax] I could put my hands on and placed it where the piece of lead was to have been. The result was immediately obvious: a great increase in the radioactivity induced in the target by the neutron beam. [Fermi]

And so on to the Nobel Prize in 1938. But why did Fermi, the most rational of scientists, make the switch? Einstein called it *Fingerspitzengefuhl*, a feeling at the tips of one's fingers, and considered it to be essential to scientific enquiry. As he put it, "There is no logical path to the elementary laws, but only intuition, resting on empathy gained by experience."

Another extraordinary example of this "obscure knowledge" is contained in Heisenberg's autobiographical account in *Physics and Beyond* of how he stumbled upon the mysterious matrices that underlay his discoveries in quantum mechanics. In the spring of 1925 Quantum Theory was in a mess. As Heisenberg wrote to his friend Pauli "What a misery! . . . the theory with atoms having more than one electron is such a great misery . . . physics is again very muddled!" In the middle of it all, Heisenberg went down with a terrible bout of hay-fever and retreated to the Island of Born to recuperate and to try to think things through. Suddenly at three o'clock one morning he woke up: it was all falling into place.

> I could no longer doubt the mathematical consistency and coher-
> ence of the kind of quantum mechanics to which my calculations
> pointed. At first, I was deeply alarmed. I had the feeling that,
> through the surface of atomic phenomena, I was looking at a
> strangely beautiful interior, and felt almost giddy at the thought
> that I now had to probe this wealth of mathematical structures that
> nature had so generously spread out before me." [Heisenberg,
> 1971]

Heisenberg had, in his dream state, rediscovered and creatively applied the Matrix theory, which he had first learned some twenty years earlier as a student.

This same sense of awe was touched on by Roger Penrose when he wrote in his *Shadows of the Mind*:

> There is something in the mystery of the way that quantum
> mechanics operates that at least seems much closer than the classi-
> cal physics, to the kind of mystery needed to accommodate mental-
> ity within the world of physical reality. [Penrose, 1995]

With the further exploration of depth psychology, of deeper clinical work, of psychopathology, the advances in psychobiology and in the chemistry and functioning of the brain—all this has led to new understandings of the relationship of psyche and soma. Now that Spirit, and even God, have made a cautious reappearance in the lexicons of the world's physicists we have to accustom ourselves to a universe in which the individual particles that make it up seem to have complete knowledge not only of their own tracks, but also of all their fellow particles back to the Big Bang. But the future life of the particles that make us up will remain, I am happy to discover, indeterminate. And with that indeterminacy we will, it seems, retain the ability to make our own path forward. Even if the past was ordained, the path to the future remains to be found. Which takes me back to James Roose-Evans's maxim that I started out with: that the best way to make a path is to keep walking.

References

Bion, W. R. (1970). *Attention and Interpretation*. London: Tavistock [reprinted London: Karnac, 1984].

Eigen, M. (1998). *The Psychoanalytic Mystic*. London: Free Association Press.

Eliade, M. (1960). *Myths, Dreams and Mysteries*. London: Harvill Press.

Evans Pritchard, E. (1940). *Nuer Religion*. New York: Oxford University Press.

Heisenberg, W. (1971). *Physics and Beyond*. London: Allen & Unwin.

Jung, C. G., & Pauli, W. (1952). Synchronicity: an acausal connecting principle. *CW* 8. London: Routledge.

Pauli, W. Unpublished correspondence.

Penrose, R. (1995). *Shadows of the Mind*. New York: Vintage.

Zinkin, L. (1987). The hologram as a model for analytical psychology. *Journal of Analytical Psychology*, 32(1).

RESPONSE BY STEVEN MENDOZA

After I read Dr Gordon's paper I looked in Lao Tzu for words that express in their own way her theme of making a path by walking.

The way is empty yet use will not drain it.
Deep it is like the ancestor of the myriad creatures.
Blunt the sharpness, untangle the knots, soften the glare.
Let your wheels move only along old ruts.
Darkly visible it only seems as if it were there.
I know not whose son it is.
It images the forefather of God.

[Lao Tzu, 1963, p. 8]

In anticipation of her paper I sought out passages that would contribute to her themes. We start with Bion, who has what may be a unique account of the psychoanalytic nature of spirituality and the conditions for it:

. . . It is quite common for psycho-analytic students to observe patients whose references to God betray the operation of

11

"memories" of the father. The term "God" is seen to indicate the scale by which the magnitude, wisdom and strength of the father is to be measured. If the psycho-analyst preserved an open mind to the mental phenomena unfolding in the psychoanalytical experience . . . he would not be restricted to interpretations of God as displaying a distorted view of the father, but would be able to assess evidence, should it present itself, for supposing that the analysand was incapable of direct experience of God and that experience of God had not occurred, because it was made impossible by the . . . degree to which memory → and ← desire obstruct the patient's relationship to an absent breast or penis on a level of mind, or at a time of life, when such an object would be so important as to evoke feelings analogous to what would in an adult be religious awe. This could be represented by desire. Taking the evidence in its other aspect, the sense memory, its significance would be its disclosure to the extent to which the patient's relationship with God was disturbed by sensuously desired models (or C category elements) which prevented an ineffable experience by their concreteness and therefore unsuitability to represent the realization. [Bion, 1967, pp. 144–145]

So Bion proposes that "references to God" do not always betoken processes which "betray the operation of 'memories' of the father" but only when his "open mind to the mental phenomena unfolding in the psychoanalytical experience" shows him that "the patient's relationship with God was disturbed by sensuously desired models". But for the concreteness of these sensuously desired models, he suggests, there is "an ineffable experience of the patient's relationship with God".

Here, perhaps, we see something of the dialogue between Pauli and Huxley that Dr Gordon referred to, about how symbols would not do justice to the depth from which the spiritual, as against the material, aspect of things was coming. This principal of disturbance by sensuously desired models pertains to what Dr Gordon emphasized about how, certainly for the Nuer people and most likely for us, the spiritual is not something that can be known through the senses.

Through the idea of the disturbance caused by "sensuously desired models" we can see the potential for a psychoanalytic understanding of celibacy in spiritual practice, not for moral reasons, but for the purpose that in psychoanalysis is called abstinence. Maybe the importance of unsaturation is the quietness and emptiness of mind that is needed to provide a potential space in which an emotional experience can evolve intuitively in atonement with ultimate reality, or "O". There is no sensual noise to drown awareness of a subtle impression and no strong impression to prejudice the emergence of the object, the evolution of the experience. Bion continues:

> In religious terms, this experience would seem to be represented by statements that the erring race or individual allowed itself to be beguiled by graven images, idols, religious statuary, or, in psychoanalysis, the idealized analyst. Interpretations should be given, based on the recognition of desire, but not that they should be derived and given from recognition of the sense memory. The need for such appreciation and interpretation is far reaching. It would extend psycho-analytic theory to cover the views of mystics from the *Bhagavad Gita* to the present. The psycho-analyst accepts the reality of reverence and awe, the possibility of a disturbance in the individual which makes atonement and, therefore, an expression of reverence and awe impossible. [*ibid.*, p. 145]

Reverence and awe are psychologically real and the psychoanalyst accepts this and with it the possibility of a disturbance, presumably of a transferential kind, that ties the patient to the false god of an idealized father and prevents him from finding real reverence and awe in a process of becoming at one (atonement) instead of merely being overawed by an imposing, but projected father figure. Here it seems that Bion is making a polemical demand on classical psychoanalysis to recognize that it is not always the father and the Oedipus complex but sometimes something that needs to be thought of both as from the depths of the self and yet also external. My understanding of spirituality is that reverence and awe are real experiences and experiences as real as our cognizance of the physical world. Substance—material, atoms, molecules—are real, unless you look too closely and then all you see are Chinese boxes. Bion concludes:

> The central postulate is that atonement with ultimate reality, or O . . . is essential to harmonious mental growth. It follows that

interpretation involves elucidation of evidence touching atonement, and not evidence only of the continuing operation of
immature relationship with a father. [Bion 1967, pp. 144–145]

I am disinclined to leave a discussion of "O" without reference
to the Buddhist doctrine of emptiness. The coincidence of this
ancient practice with Bion's ideas suggests a body of potential
psychoanalytic knowledge latent in cultures that have had longer
to gain experience than the century of psychoanalysis. What is
empty in emptiness is not the annihilation that nineteenth-century
academic accounts of nirvana presumed emptiness to mean, but the
emptiness of inherent existence. This means that the world as we
see it is held in this doctrine to be a mere appearance to mind lacking inherent existence, constructed as mental phenomena. This is
similar to the principle of psychic reality and the need for projective identification to reach out and put a world out there for us.
What is paradoxical about the practice of emptiness is that this dual
view of objects both as they appear to mind and as lacking inherent existence is a more aesthetic experience for being philosophi-
cally valid. The sensory impact of what we know to be subjective is
more vivid and immediate and meaningful than the deluded view
of the world as actually being as we see it.

This realization of emptiness includes a realization of the emptiness of the self of inherent existence. This can be a terrifying experience. To know ourselves as subjects having experience but not as
objects saturated with qualities offers very little defence against the
threat of psychic annihilation. Hence Bion's references to sense and
memory being evoked in the wrong direction by the absence of an
object.

There is a fragment of Bion which is essential:

It may be wondered what state of mind is welcome if desires and
memory are not. A term that would express approximately what I
need to express is "faith"—faith that there is an ultimate reality and
truth—the unknown, unknowable, "formless infinite". [Bion, 1970,
p. 31]

Now we go on to two instances of manifestations of the spirit
that Dr Gordon points out is missing from contemporary culture:

the first is from a rather scurrilous explorer called Redmond O'Hanlon. Here he is on a terrifying journey he made in the Congo, a journey literally to the heart of darkness, to the same territory that Conrad wrote about:

> A soft but persistent rain began to patter on the canvas. I turned off the precious batteries, lay on my side with two mould-rotted shirts under my hip and a pair of pants for a pillow, and half-dreamed about Darwin's cousin, Francis Galton, pioneer geneticist and statistician, father of the anti-cyclone and finger-printing, and anticipator of the Freudian unconscious. Using the technique he invented, the word-association test, he would take a dictionary. write out 100 words all beginning with 'a' on separate slips of paper, hide them under a book so that only their edges peeped out, draw one at random, start a stopwatch, and give himself four seconds to produce as many responses as he could. He found it a surprisingly difficult, repugnant process—and when he published his results in the journal *Brain*, in 1879, he excused himself from detailing his actual associations, from describing images that no gentleman could disclose, because they "lay bare the foundation of a man's thought with curious distinctness, and exhibit his mental anatomy with more vividness and truth than he would probably care to publish to the world". [O'Hanlon, 1997]

He concluded that perhaps

> the strongest impression left by these experiments regards the multifariousness of the work done by the mind in a state of half unconsciousness, and the valid reason they afford for believing in the existence of still deeper strata of mental operations, sunk wholly below the level of consciousness, which may account for such mental phenomena as cannot otherwise be explained. [*ibid.*]

This was a good ten years before Freud used free association to discover or create or invent his version of the unconscious (Freud subscribed to *Brain* and he refers to papers by the neurologist Hughlings Jackson in the January and October issues of 1879, although perhaps he missed Galton's article and he certainly never acknowledged his priority).

But it was one of Galton's outwardly most trivial experiments which filled my mind as I fell asleep. Fascinated by the so-called worship of idols, he decided to investigate its mechanism, so he cast around for an entirely inappropriate image and settled on Mr. Punch. He pinned a cover of the journal up in his study and forced himself to make obeisance every morning, derailing his fears, whispering his hopes, until the experiment began to work so well he had to stop. Each time he entered his club and caught a glimpse of Mr. Punch lying in state on the periodicals table his mouth went dry, his legs became unsteady, and a sweat broke out across his shoulders. Here in the forest, I thought, there seemed no mystery at all about the power of Mr. Punch. [O'Hanlon, 1997, pp. 357–358]

We go on to a rather similar story by Alexandra David-Neel from her journeys in Tibet:

The second story has all the appearances of having been invented by a miscreant joker to ridicule the devotees, but it is not so. No one in Tibet finds it laughable or irreverent. The fact related is accepted as revealing a strict truth about all cults. Whatever it may be, the worshipped object is only possessed with the power, which is supplied to it by the collective concentration of thoughts and the faith of its worshippers.

The aged mother of a trader who went each year to India, asked her son to bring her a relic from the Holy Land. The trader promised to do so, but his mind being much occupied with the cares of his business, he forgot his promise.

The old woman felt very sad, and the next year, when her son's caravan started again, she renewed her request for the holy relic.

Again the trader promised to bring one, and again he forgot it. The same thing happened for the third time the following year. However, this time the merchant remembered his promise before reaching his home and was much troubled at the idea of once more disappointing his aged mother's eager expectation.

As he pondered over the matter, seeking a way to mend his neglect, he caught sight of a piece of a dog's jaw lying near the road.

A sudden inspiration came to him. He broke off a tooth of the bleached jaw-bone, wiped away the earth which covered it and wrapped it in a piece of silk. Then, having reached his house, he offered the old bone to his mother, declaring that it was a most precious relic, a tooth of the great Sariputra.

Overjoyed, her heart filled with veneration, the good woman placed the tooth in a casket on the altar of the family shrine: Each day she worshipped before it, lighting lamps and burning incense. Other devotees joined in the worship and after a time rays of light shone from the dog's tooth, promoted holy relic.

A popular Tibetan saying is born from that story . . . which means 'If there is veneration even a dog's tooth emits light.'
Once more we see that Tibetan theories about all phenomena are always the same at heart. All are grounded on the power of the mind and this is only logical for people who consider the world, as we see it, to be but a subjective vision. [David-Neel, 1929, p. 212]

I hope that the material I have quoted shows how Bion has tried to account for the spirit being missing in psychoanalysis and how, through a careful distinction of the patient remembering a sensuous object from the patient desiring a non-sensuous one, it may be recovered. I hope the latter quotations show the intensity of the spirit and how delicate is the balance between the sensuous and the spiritual.

References

Bion, W. (1967). *Second Thoughts*. London: Heinemann [reprinted London: Karnac, 1984].

Bion, W. (1970). *Attention and Interpretation*. London: Tavistock [reprinted London: Karnac, 1984].

David-Neel, A. (1937). *Magic and Mystery in Tibet*. London: Souvenir Press.

O'Hanlon, R. (1997). *Congo Journey*. London: Penguin Books.

Tzu, Lao (1963). *Tao Te Ching*, D. C. Lau (Trans.). London: Penguin Books.

The challenge of evolution and the place of sympathy

David M. Black

Preface

I n considering the topic of "Psychotherapy and spirituality" I soon came to realize that one specific question particularly interested me. It was, essentially: can we find a use for the word spirituality, or for its meaning, in a scientific age? Richard Dawkins in *The Selfish Gene* quotes with approval a zoologist who asked the question: "What is man?" and answered: ". . . all attempts to answer that question before 1859 are worthless, and we will be better off if we ignore them completely" (Dawkins, 1976). 1859 was the date of Darwin's *Origin of Species*. Such "scientism" may strike us as naïve, but with the ever-increasing power that science gives us over the life and death of our species it is important to be in touch with the truth it contains. Therefore, instead of talking about spiritual questions in general, I shall address this one question, of spirituality and science, in particular.

Introduction

The excellent science writer and palaeontologist, the late Stephen Jay Gould, recently published a book entitled *Rocks of Ages*, in which he argued that science and religion need in no way be in conflict (Gould, 2001). Science and religion, he said, are two entirely separate domains of intellectual authority, two "non-overlapping magisteria" as he majestically put it, and the religionist and the scientist are each free to go about their business without in any way needing to glance over their shoulder to see what the other is up to.

This can't be right, in my view. Religions are bound to make reality claims—indeed, perhaps the profoundest of all reality claims—and therefore, like the sciences, they are bound to be interested in all the questions to do with our knowledge of reality. Such questions are: how do we know what we know?; what persuades us that something is true?; what do we regard as evidence?; how can we tell—and *can* we tell?—what is delusion and what is truth-telling? All these questions, known by philosophers under the heading of epistemology, set us thinking about the impact of the growth of the scientific mind upon religion, and in particular on our thinking about spirituality. Spirituality is a vague term with many meanings. It is, in origin, a metaphor from a world-view that few of us now subscribe to. But I want to address in particular one rather important and specific meaning: what gives force and stability to values? I shall have fulfilled my intention in this paper if I can show that there may be a place, in a scientific world-view, for values that have force and stability in their own right and are not merely subservient to the *real politico* of evolution.

Background: Galileo's "primary qualities"

In June 1633 Pope Urban VIII ordered the "rigorous examination" of Galileo by the Inquisition. Galileo was sixty-nine; he had already been twice examined by the Inquisition; he was under "vehement suspicion of heresy"; and he knew that "rigorous examination" involved torture, with the threat of being burned alive if he was found guilty. If you want to claim any one man as the originator of the modern scientific mind, I think you would be bound to select Galileo. To this day, if you read his account of discovering that the moon has mountains and valleys, like the earth, and is not the perfectly smooth sphere required by Ptolemaic astronomy you sense that lovely quality of modern science, the absolute attention to the facts of observation, and the careful process of discussion of how best they can be understood. The outcome of such discussion can give the scientist a sense of revelation comparable to a religious experience. And, when you hear that he was threatened with being burned alive, you may remember that Galileo had already given some thought to heat. In his essay, *The Assayer*, he had suggested that heat is one of those qualities that have no real existence except inside us; outside ourselves they are mere names. He had written:

> Those materials which produce heat in us, and make us feel warmth, which are known by the general name of "fire", would then be a multitude of minute particles having certain shapes and moving with certain velocities. Meeting with our bodies, they penetrate by means of their extreme subtlety, and their touch as felt by us when they pass through our substance is the sensation we call "heat". This is pleasant or unpleasant according to the greater or smaller speed of these particles as they go pricking and penetrating; pleasant when this assists our necessary transpiration, and obnoxious when it causes too great a separation and dissolution of our substance. [Drake, 1957].

Galileo was wrong about the physics of heat, as it happens, but he was right about its obnoxiousness. Confronted with the threat of torture, he recanted, and lived for the rest of his life under house arrest in Florence.

What he was getting at in his account of heat, however, was the distinction that was taken up by John Locke and that would underlie the whole of science for the next 400 years. This was the distinction between the primary qualities of matter, which are the objectively measurable, such as dimension, mass, velocity, acceleration, etc; and the secondary qualities, which depend on our sense organs and include such things as colour, smell, sound, sweetness, and heat. This distinction is so profound, and so far-reaching in its effects, that it takes time to realize its implications. One was that a world of primary qualities could be grasped exactly by mathematics. We are still discovering the power of that grasp.

What was the intellectual picture that Galileo was disturbing? It was that remarkable synthesis of Christian theology and classical Greek thought that Thomas Aquinas had put together in the thirteenth century, and that dominated the universities of Europe for the next 450 years. It is usually known as Aristotelian scholasticism, and in it the word "spirit" has a clear literal meaning. The fundamental question here is whether it can have any meaning in any other world-view. Aristotelian scholasticism is a system characterised by strongly vertical relations. God is above his Creation, man is above the beasts, the monarch is above his subjects, men are above women, and the Ancients are above the Moderns. The individual human is torn between his spirit, which aspires upward, and his base desires, which threaten to drag him down into the world and the flesh. Spirit is one sort of stuff, and spiritual beings like souls and angels are made of it; matter is another sort of stuff, and material things like stones and loaves of bread are made of matter.

One of the ways in which this system seems most strange to us is that the past had authority over the present. If you wanted to know what you should believe, you didn't rely on your own experience or your own judgment; you turned first to the proper Authority, which was Scripture, the Word of God, which was always correct if sometimes obscure; and second to the other designated authorities, the Church Fathers and certain great pagan philosophers, above all Aristotle. The proper use of reason was to "deduce from Authority" what was the case; it was not to "induce", to use the technical word, what was the case from the facts around you.

This attitude is so unlike the way we imagine we think nowadays that it is easy to pillory it. In practice, it still applies. Even today, most responsible scientists think many times before departing from their designated authorities and venture to rely on their own perceptions. This conservatism is the condition on which what Thomas Kuhn calls "normal science" can be practised (Kuhn, 1962). The *Journal of the American Psychoanalytic Association* recently published an early paper by an eminent psychoanalyst, the late Robert Stoller, describing apparently telepathic dreams relating to his patients; Stoller had taken the advice of his supervisor, Ralph Greenson, and buried the paper for forty years in a desk drawer. He didn't fear being burned at the stake, but he did fear, in the climate of American psychoanalysis in the 1960s, that such a paper could destroy his budding career (Mayer, 2001). Professional opinion, like the obnoxiousness of fire, is a force to be reckoned with. The Ptolemaic picture of the heavens was part of the Aristotelian scholastic world-view. The heavenly bodies, being higher than the earth, were more perfect than the earth, and part of their perfection was that they moved in perfectly circular orbits and were themselves perfect spheres. When Galileo built his telescope, and saw for the first time that the shadows of mountains on the moon were longer at dawn, and shorter at noon, exactly like the shadows of mountains on earth, it was suddenly clear that scholastic theory was vulnerable to empirical attack. When Galileo went on to declare that the primary qualities of the world were those that could be measured, and all other qualities were secondary, he inverted the entire diagram of Aristotelian scholasticism. Suddenly the Authorities of the past were only people like us, who made mistakes like us, and all because they had not recognized the importance of setting observation and measurement alongside speculation and reflection. Francis Bacon, Galileo's contemporary, who had been trained in Aristotelian scholasticism, came to refer contemptuously to Aristotle and the Church Fathers as the "Idols of the Lecture-Theatre".

In the course of the seventeenth century Bacon, Descartes, Locke, Newton, and many others built on these revolutionary insights that Galileo had introduced. Intellectually, it was a hugely exciting time, and the changes that resulted, which are usually called the Enlightenment or the Scientific Revolution, are among the most fundamental in the history of human thought. There is a tendency at present among postmodernist thinkers to speak as if a scientific world-view is just one intellectual option among others, as if the Pope and Galileo might equally be right. That position, I think, is untenable. Yet, at the same time, Galileo was attempting to do something very curious, to construe a world devoid of human sensibility, so it is possible to sympathize with the Pope's misgivings. To hold a scientific world-view doesn't commit you to any particular scientific theory, but it does commit you to certain methods of argument and to certain basic rules about what constitutes evidence for the truth or falsity of propositions. Freud once discussed the question of whether psychoanalysis entails a distinctive *Weltanschauung* of its own. He concluded that it did not: its world-view is the ordinary scientific one. That seems to me correct, and it is why in this paper I am talking mainly about science in general, and not psychoanalysis in particular.

So, one of our first questions about spirituality is: does this notion, which occupied a comprehensible place in the Aristotelian scholastic world-view, have any place in a scientific one? Galileo himself, like Stephen Jay Gould, saw no problem, and he stated his position with his characteristic energy: the Holy Bible and the phenomena of nature proceed alike, he said, from the divine Word. The Holy Spirit is not concerned to teach us whether the heavens move or stand still; its goal is our salvation, and if we take an interest in these lesser matters then we must read God's other book, the Book of Nature, in which truths are also to be found. Truths cannot contradict one another, he argued, and there can be no danger that the discoveries of science will overthrow "the dignity and majesty of Scripture" (Letter to Grand Duchess Christina, 1615, in Drake, 1957). As the seventeenth century proceeded, however, and the spectacular advances, which Galileo's commonsensical attitudes made possible, were applied to the Bible itself, they began to reveal factual inconsistencies in the Gospels, and the moral inconsistency between God's teachings and his apparent government of the world. For example, if God favoured the mass murderer and adulterer King David, what exactly made us hold God up as a moral exemplar? The divine story lost credibility; the laws of Nature seemed to operate reliably without divine intervention; and in the following century witty, irreverent thinkers like Voltaire and David Hume suggested that if God needed to intervene in his universe, it must be because he had made a botch of designing it in the first place. Rational thinkers moved towards Deism, which kept a place for God as initiator of the universe, but rejected the messy particulars, as they came to seem, of the Christian revelation. The world of matter and the world of mind, *res extensa* and *res cogitans* as Descartes called them, were clearly distinct, and as long as that was the case, it was possible to think that mankind was in some sense a "separate creation" from the rest of the world, subject to different laws and intended for a different and higher purpose. In the first two and a half centuries after Galileo, spirituality retained a place, essentially because no one could wholly connect the world of man with the world of nature. And there was always also a countercurrent of hostility to the triumphal march of Galilean science. At the end of the eighteenth century the poets Goethe in Germany, and William Blake in England, both passionately opposed Newton's explanation of light. Their objections were misguided, but they deserve respect. The elimination of human subjectivity from the scientific account of the world aroused severe, not yet quite explainable, misgivings.

The challenge of evolution

In many ways, by the end of the eighteenth century the intellectual world could foresee the inevitability of making the connection between man and nature. Between 1790 and 1810 Goethe, Darwin's grandfather, Erasmus, Lamarck, and Schopenhauer all put forward evolutionary theories. But none of them could quite work out a convincing mechanism for the process they were glimpsing. Lamarck's version of evolution, which involved the inheritance of acquired characteristics, is described by one disapproving modern commentator as "downright spiritual; it featured an inexorable tendency toward greater organic complexity and more highly conscious life." (Wright, 1994).

Every historian of evolution discusses the reasons for "Darwin's delay"—the twenty years that Darwin waited before publishing his theory of evolution and the origin of species by natural selection alone. Perhaps it isn't hard to understand. Darwin no longer had to fear the fires of the Inquisition, but he was a gentle and cautious man with a hugely bold and tenacious mind, and he could see what the implications of his theory were. By revealing a natural mechanism that could account for the origin of all species, including mankind, he was annihilating, at a stroke, the whole base on which a "spiritual" view of the universe, and of man's place and purpose within it, depended. After publishing *The Origin of Species*, he waited a further twelve years before publishing *The Descent of Man*. There, he shows his very clear perception that henceforth we had to account for the so-called spiritual qualities of human beings—the capacities for love, conscience, the pursuit of knowledge, and so on—by linking their origin with the evolutionary imperatives of survival and reproduction. In his view there was no other source for life's characteristics.

With Darwin we arrive at the sharp point of the attack made by "materialism" upon "spirituality", by "science" upon "religion". Contrary to Lamarck, nothing is passed down from one generation to another unless it can get through the narrow gate of the genes.

Everything is accounted for without remainder by the random events of sexual selection in an unstable environment subject in principle to unpredictable catastrophe.

All this was deeply shocking to Christians raised with a belief that God cares for every sparrow that falls to the earth. But further reflection revealed an even more disturbing implication of Darwin's theory. If our brains, and all our capacities, have been shaped by the arbitrary requirements of survival and reproduction, then that applies also to our emotions and our thinking processes. Far from being created to give us access to the truth, they have emerged for one reason only, namely that they enabled our predecessors to cope with the competition. Morality and sincerity, our most precious attributes, if they primarily served the purpose of survival of the species, may be a veil of illusion and self-deception thrown over our acts, not by reprehensible hypocrisy, but by our genes. A well-known modern Darwinian has put the matter in precisely these terms. Living organisms, Richard Dawkins has said, are nothing but "survival machines" designed to fulfil the purposes of self-replicating complex molecules, namely the DNA that makes up our genes (Dawkins, 1976).

I think the crucial question I want to ask emerges clearly: if we humans, like the giraffe and the albatross, exist solely because natural selection in its infinite and meaningless vicissitudes has produced us—and that includes our thinking, our emotions, our senses, and all our capacities for experience, from the squalid to the mystical—what weight can we put on any of it? As Freud said, the ego is first and foremost a body ego; we do indeed derive from our genes, and the one certainty any of us can have about our countless ancestors is that, whether they were bacteria or fish or lemurs, they all found ways to reproduce themselves and to survive in the ever-changing environment of earth. This does not mean, however, that human beings are wholly determined by their genes. Richard Dawkins' metaphor, the "selfish gene", is a neat way of dramatizing his point, but it remains no more than a metaphor. Genes are molecules, they are incapable of selfishness or of having purposes. Living organisms may resemble machines in some respects, but they are not machines. A machine is something built to fulfil the purposes of an organism; an organism does not come into existence to fulfil the purposes of any agency outside itself. The danger of

Dawkins' metaphor, in itself harmless, is that it invites us to admire the gene and despise the organism. These points are hard to formulate in a scientific context, and the reason takes us straight back to Galileo and the distinction between primary and secondary qualities. Science has made such gigantic strides, by focusing exclusively on primary qualities, that it has come to seem unscientific to attend to the secondary ones. Yet it is worth noticing that Galileo forswore his theories when threatened with the fires of the Inquisition. It was not their primary qualities that concerned him. What he recoiled from was precisely their secondary qualities, what he called the "obnoxiousness" of heat. Human motivation is very often determined by secondary qualities that depend on, but can't be reduced to, primary ones. The fear that many people have expressed about the spectacular progress of modern science is in touch with a real danger: that to privilege the primary qualities risks down-grading the crucial importance of those that are called secondary. What Galileo proved was that systems of primary qualities are understood best if we think only in terms of primary qualities. That establishes nothing about other systems.

The place of sympathy

One inescapable fact about human beings is that we are born prematurely, and spend our first months in a condition of extreme dependence. This is usually said to be because the human head is so large, to accommodate its brain, that if the baby were not born early it would be unable to pass through the birth canal. Perhaps because of the great sensitivity that being a baby, and looking after a baby, require, human beings—women especially—have developed an extraordinary capacity for sympathy. I want to rescue this word from its diminished modern meaning of pity, and give it the central and fundamental position it deserves. Sympathy has been disparaged in psychotherapeutic discussion; empathy is often said where sympathy is meant. Sympathy is our capacity to be in touch with, and care about, the feelings of others; psychoanalytically we can think of it, as Melanie Klein said of empathy, as starting from a projection of our own feelings. But we are a social species and the universality of our emotional expressions (documented by

Darwin) suggests that we have an in-built preparedness to recognize emotion in another. Sympathy should be distinguished from the synthetic word "empathy", which is based on the separateness of human beings, and emphasizes the psychological use that can be made of a trial identification with the other. Sympathy is an immediate feeling response to the imagined feeling of the other, and it is the necessary base not only of actions evoking kindness, but also of actions involving cruelty.

Darwin describes sympathy as "all-important". He perceives it in animals, including elephants and monkeys, and gives it a central place in our life. He sees the combination of sympathy with our capacities for memory and reflection as lying behind our distinctive humanity, writing:

> Even when we are quite alone, how often do we think with pleasure or pain of what others think of us—of their imagined approbation or disapprobation; and this all follows from *sympathy*, a fundamental element of the social instincts. A man who possessed no trace of such instincts would be an unnatural monster. [Darwin, 1871, p. 112, my italics]

Darwin is describing here our essentially social disposition, which means that, even when we are alone, people close to us or from our past are always present. The word empathy cannot embrace this ever-present awareness of the opinions and feelings of others.

The importance Darwin ascribes to sympathy is very striking, and has largely been ignored by subsequent thinkers. Since the 1960s, however, there has been a revival of interest in the general idea that so preoccupied Freud: that evolution must also be responsible for our mental capacities. Modern biologists, who now use computers to model the influence of mutations through hundreds of generations, have shown that a capacity for what is called "reciprocal altruism" gives a huge evolutionary advantage over populations in which all compete against all. Reciprocal altruism is a strategy in which I treat you well initially, and then respond to you according to the way you treat me. If you treat me well, I treat you well; if you treat me badly I treat you badly. Organisms that follow this strategy do much better than organisms that follow the strategy, that many early evolutionists took for granted, of hostile competition in all circumstances (Dawkins, 1976; Sulloway, 1998).

This recognition that altruism, albeit with limitations, makes evolutionary sense allows us to enter a new world of thought about human motivation. Many people dislike these evolutionary arguments, because they seem so mechanical and "calculating", but that is because they are put in misleadingly intellectual form. The altruistic chimpanzee does not come to the aid of a formerly friendly chimpanzee with a view to getting help from him in the future, in order to preserve his genes: on the contrary, he simply has certain *feelings* towards another who has helped him. We tend to like those who are friendly and helpful to us, and to dislike those who are not. Liking and friendship are what guide us to have helpful attitudes towards another; dislike and antagonism are what push us in the opposite direction. We are selected to have feelings, not thoughts (Wright, 1994).

These developments in the modern understanding of evolution are enormously far-reaching. But to arrive at the issues specific to spirituality, I want to return briefly to the notion of sympathy, and then to the transformation of the human species, in comparison with all others, by the development of language. Humans may not be a "special creation" apart from the rest of the evolutionary process, but we have to a huge extent been created by a unique process that does not flow through the genes, and which no other animal shares. To put the subject matter of evolution in terms of *feelings* such as liking and disliking is a radical step forward. What Galileo called the secondary qualities are reinstated as of scientific importance. We neither like nor dislike the primary qualities, as such, but the secondary qualities, the beauty of a smile or the obnoxiousness of fire, affect us profoundly and guide our actions in crucial ways.

Such feelings, however, remain external to the other: they affect us, but they may tell us little about him. Sympathy relates us to the other in an entirely different way. Our sympathy is with the subjectivity of the other. Freud spoke of consciousness, in what still seems to me a most admirable definition, as "a sense-organ for the perception of psychic qualities" (Freud, 1900a; Black, 2001; see also Solms, 1997). We might say, in parallel, that sympathy is a sense-organ for the perception of psychic qualities in others. Through sympathy we know, or imagine we know, what it is like to be the other; we can care as much, in a moment of sympathy, for the other's welfare as for our own. In psychoanalytic language, in the moment of sympathy we identify with the other, and I have suggested (Black, 2001) that the origin for this capacity lies in the intensity of emotions between mother and baby. Those emotions are hugely important, and they make possible appropriate action, whether it is practical, such as feeding, or playful, with all the mental and neurological enhancement that play so lightly carries. Sympathy, the awareness of the inwardness of the other, is a source of knowledge, although, of course, like all perceptions it is far from fool-proof and needs to be reality-tested. I am avoiding technical terms like intersubjectivity, projective identification, mentalization, and so on because I want to stress the wordless immediacy and simplicity of sympathy. The language of psychoanalysis still carries its Freudian legacy of emphasizing human separateness; human beings are physically separate, of course, but with sympathy we are reminded of how fundamentally we are also social.

The impact of language on sympathy

I come now to the final step in this argument. Sympathy can be observed among many animals and birds in relation to their young and their mates. Darwin describes it in monkeys and elephants; and Loren Eiseley has a moving story of the ecstasy of a female hawk when he released her mate, whom he had captured and kept caged overnight (Eiseley, 1978). But human beings differ from other species in the altogether unique range and stability of their sympathies, and to understand this we need to bring in language, and a whole world of historical transmission that no longer depends on the mechanical imperatives of genetics.

"Words are for those with promises to keep", said W. H. Auden in his poem "Their Lonely Betters" (Auden, 1966). I think what he meant was that words are for those who try to give stability to their world of feeling. Freud gave a very special place to words. It is by their interposition, as he put it, that "internal thought-processes are made into perceptions" (Freud, 1923b). They are what enable the incoherent chaos of unconscious wishing to acquire unity, purpose, and duration (qualities of the ego, in his language). More recently, Ronald Britton has shown that the "beliefs" that give reality to internal objects can only be altered if they are first brought into consciousness and thought about (Britton, 1998). This process requires the clarity of verbal thought. No doubt we can think, in some sense, without words; but for clarity of thought, for really "knowing what we think" (and what we don't), words are the indispensable tools.

Left to its own devices, sympathy is a transient and fickle thing, easily obliterated by other emotions such as disgust or socially-sanctioned prejudice. It is also a wordless thing, an affective talent continuous with our pre-human past. Coupled with language, however, it becomes the subject of what Darwin called reflection; the inner lives and feelings of others become more consistently present to us, as they are for themselves. This process allows the development of a sense of personhood and gradually of obligation and law, of what constitutes fulfilment of the law, and what constitutes violation of it. It builds up over many generations, and it isn't conceivable that it could build up in an individual in a single lifetime. One of the interesting functions of religious intuition is that it sometimes makes a sort of premonitory registration of this deepening sympathetic insight. Jefferson, in the "Declaration of Independence", proclaimed that all men were endowed by their Creator with certain inalienable rights, apparently not noticing as he did so that he was surrounded by slaves whose rights had very clearly been alienated. Gradually, the implicit awareness of human and animal rights, and the lofty concern attributed to God, have been withdrawn from projection and begun to be felt on the pulses of actual human beings. A modern Jefferson would abhor slavery.

Developments of this sort are inconceivable without language, and perhaps specifically written language, used in a continuing tradition over many generations. Our genes give us the necessary capacities for this process, but it can't be described as derived from or carried by them. And the sexual and other choices made by human beings, which crucially decide which genes will pass to the next generation, are profoundly influenced by factors at this cultural level. The causal chains that determine human life circle promiscuously through both "primary" and "secondary" qualities; Galileo's distinction is not helpful to us in our attempt to understand human lives.

Equally, there is no way in which we can return to the pre-Galilean world-view of Aristotelian scholasticism. There is no reason to believe in some sort of spiritual "stuff", alternative to matter, out of which "souls" are made. Words such as "spirit" and "spirituality" survive as metaphors from the pre-Galilean world-view. What we are talking about, to use more pedestrian and literal language, are emergent properties, which accrue as our sympathy, stabilized by language and cultural tradition, reaches out more widely and consistently to the denizens of our universe. The process is an ongoing and variable one, not divinely safeguarded, and always subject, like every other living process, to derailment by unforeseen events.

References

Auden, W. H. (1966). *Collected Shorter Poems*. London: Faber and Faber.

Black, D. M. (2001). Psychoanalysis and the function of consciousness. In: A. Molino (Ed.), *Where Id Was: Challenging Normalization in Psychoanalysis*. London: Continuum.

Britton, R. (1998). Belief and psychic reality. In: *Belief and Imagination*. London: Routledge.

Darwin, C. (1871). *The Descent of Man*. London: John Murray.

Dawkins, R (1976). *The Selfish Gene*. Oxford: Oxford University Press.

Drake, S. (1957). *Discoveries and Opinions of Galileo (Selected Translated Writings)*. New York: Random House.

Eiseley, L. (1978). *The Star Thrower*. New York: Harcourt Brace Jovanovich.

Freud, S. (1900a). Interpretation of dreams. *S.E.*, 4–5.

Freud, S. (1923b). The ego and the id. *S.E.*, 19

Gould, S. J. (2001). *Rocks of Ages*. London: Jonathan Cape.

Kuhn, T. (1962). *The Structure of Scientific Revolutions*. Chicago: University of Chicago Press.

Mayer, E. L. (2001). On "telepathic dreams"? An unpublished paper by Robert J. Stoller. *Journal of the American Psychoanalytic Association*, 49(2).

Solms, M. (1997). What is consciousness? *Journal of the American Psychoanalytic Association*, 45(4).

Sulloway, F. (1998). Darwinian virtues. *New York Review of Books*, 9 April.

Wright, R. (1994). *The Moral Animal*. London: Abacus.

RESPONSE BY ADRIAN DICKINSON

David Black's paper takes us on a huge trajectory, an intellectual and emotional journey that leads back to past controversies in order to find a place for spirituality in a post-Darwinian age. In fact, he goes back as far as Galileo, who initiated the scientific method by making a basic distinction between the primary qualities of matter and the secondary qualities of subjective experience. This relegation of our inner experience, which includes religious belief, to a secondary status carries the implication that it is not "real" in the way that matter is real. So it is little wonder that Galileo was threatened with torture and death by the Catholic Church.

The major scientific assault on the foundations of religious faith came later, with the publication of Darwin's *Origin of Species* in 1859, and continues to the present day. David Black quotes a contemporary zoologist who responded to the question: "What is man?" with the comment: ". . . all attempts to answer that question before 1859 are worthless, and we will be better off if we ignore them completely". Black comments that such "scientism may strike us as naïve . . . but it is important to be in touch with the truth it contains". Spirituality, he observes, is a vague term with many meanings: a metaphor derived from a world view "that few people now subscribe to". His aim in this paper, he says, is to show that there is a place, in a scientific world view, for values which have force and stability in their own right and are not merely subservient to the *realpolitik* of evolution.

Black himself concludes that Galileo's distinction between what he called primary and secondary qualities may be important in the history of science but is "not helpful to us in our attempt to understand human lives". He goes on to challenge Dawkins' "selfish gene" theory that human beings are wholly determined by their genes, with the succinct comment that "genes can't be selfish because they are molecules". But, much as I am impressed by David Black's aim to rescue values from the destructive grip of science—which he tackles with admirable erudition and enthusiasm—I think he fails in his attempt to divorce human values from the *realpolitik* of evolution, or of the scientific world view. His argument seems to leave us in a position that whatever is evolutionarily advantageous is morally good. He rightly criticizes Richard Dawkins, but then seems to give credence to Hamilton's theory of "inclusive fitness" that substitutes "genetic material" for genes. But if genes cannot be selfish, that is, have moral qualities, then genetic material cannot either. To say altruism is good because it is evolutionarily advantageous seems to me a most dubious proposition. It may be advantageous, but it crucially lacks that quality or consequence that makes it good. It seems to leave out the essence of morality, rather in the way the poet Clough satirized Victorian morality in "The Latest Decalogue" (Clough, 1862) with his version of the Sixth Commandment:

Do not adultery commit
Advantage rarely comes of it.

Moreover, if we take note of current scientific theory, the attempt to rescue human subjectivity from science may have already become redundant. Perhaps, as Rosemary Gordon suggested in her talk in this series, and David Black endorsed in part in his, the pendulum is already swinging back and science itself now seriously questions Galileo's split between subjectivity and objectivity.

In the major thrust of his argument David Black declares that "spirituality is begotten by language upon sympathy", and that it is the "no-longer-very-satisfactory name for a group of emergent properties that accrue upon the development of a language-based culture". I can see where he is coming from, and the expression of spirituality will no doubt be culture-specific, finding form in words and other symbols, but this formulation seems to lose much of what the word "spiritual" means, either etymologically or historically. The baby has been thrown out with the bath-water.

Despite David Black's criticism of Aristotelian Scholasticism I think his paper is Aristotelian in the sense of Raphael's painting of the Academy in Athens; Aristotle is depicted pointing downward, pointing to where we have come from, developmentally and historically. He is pointing to the body-ego, to Galileo's primary qualities, to genes and genetic material and to the mechanical imperatives of genetics. I think we need a balancing dose of Plato: "Plato and Aristotle!" Jung writes in *Psychological Types* "These are not merely two systems, they are types of two distinct human natures, which from time immemorial . . . stand . . . opposed" (Jung, 1971).

For the Scholastics everything in existence with any form had a soul, that is, something that kept it in existence, held it together. There was a hierarchy: mineral, vegetable, animal, human, and angelic. David Black suggests that such hierarchical thinking has gone today, but I'm not so sure that it has. The notion of higher and lower, or more developed and less developed, is still part of our thinking, with implied value judgements as well. Thus, for instance, the bedrock of Freudian psychoanalysis, the development of the ego from the id, "where id was, ego shall be", the movement from unconscious to conscious, implies a hierarchy. Winnicott, writing of "psyche-soma" (1965, p. 45), is using the language that I was brought up in: it carries the fundamental notion that man is a psychosomatic entity. And we use this hierarchy in our work as psychotherapists. Following Freud's theory of symptom conversion, we assume that if there is something in the mind that cannot be expressed, borne, or known, it may well emerge as a physical symptom, and then may disappear as that "something" is transformed from a physical to a mental level.

This idea of transformation leads naturally to Bion, whose spirit I think has been present in different forms throughout this whole lecture series. Bion is in the Platonic tradition, aware that "a curtain of illusion separates us from reality" and emphasizing that "there is a gap between phenomena and the thing-in-itself" (Bion, 1965).

For me, Bion's key concept is what he calls alpha function. Our raw sense impressions, whether from within or without, which he calls beta elements, are transformed by alpha function into alpha elements that are capable of bearing meaning, of being known, of being mentally digested. By contrast, beta elements, things-in-themselves, cannot be known but only reacted to as raw sensory stimuli.

This transformation is the key mental process. It is what makes us human and I link it with the idea of the imagination of the Romantics.

The Romantics, reacting to the nineteenth century theory of Associationism, which constituted a mechanical, stimulus-response view of the mind, asserted that imagination, or the poetic spirit, creates for each of us a living world. Without it we are dead and mechanical ourselves. Jung is of this tradition when he writes in *Memories, Dreams, Reflections* of his realization that

> man is indispensable for the completion of creation; that in fact he himself is the second creator of the world, who alone has given to the world its objective existence, without which, unheard, unseen, silently eating, giving birth, dying, heads nodding, through hundreds of millions of years, it would have gone on in the profoundest night of non-being down to its unknown end. Human consciousness created objective existence and meaning . . . [Jung, 1963]

Or, as Coleridge put it:

> O Sara, we receive but what we give
> And in our life alone does Nature live . . .
> [Dejection: A Lettter (1802)]

Wordsworth writes vividly of the origin of this poetic spirit, and here I would support David Black in his emphasis on "sympathy", for it is in sympathy, or that first feeling together of baby and mother, that life, as opposed to mere survival, starts. Wordsworth writes of the "infant babe . . . nursed in his mother's arms . . .

> —who, when his soul
> Claims manifest kindred with an earthly soul

Doth gather passion from his mother's eye.
Such feelings pass into his torpid life
Like an awakening breeze, and hence his mind . . .
Is prompt and watchful . . .

Until:

—his mind
Even as an agent of the one great mind
Creates, creator and receiver both
Working but in alliance with the works
Which it beholds. Such, verily, is the first
Poetic spirit of our human life

[Wordsworth, 1799]

Here is a poetic statement of alpha function at work; a living perception of the world comes about through feeling, as David Black himself emphasized. I think that Wordsworth here achieves a union of the Aristotelian and the Platonic by linking "the works which it beholds" and "the one great mind". The human mind, for Wordsworth, is "creator and receiver both", somehow joining the two worlds through the poetic spirit. I suspect it was this mysterious process that Donald Meltzer was referring to in an earlier talk in this series when he said he had been "reflecting a lot recently on the difference between invention and discovery".

Another way of thinking about this is to use the idea of symbolization. A symbol will in itself unite the physical and the mental, the material and the spiritual, the unconscious and the conscious. Language is its pre-eminent form; language shapes the world we live in, so that in a sense the only world we live in is the symbolic one. And this must profoundly affect our ideas of evolution, for then it does not just become a blind process of survival, but a process of active interaction with the world.

The struggle for survival becomes the struggle to make a better society.

I wonder if it was this sense of struggle that, for me, was missing from David Black's paper, with its rather passive image of the chimpanzee "being selected for" survival by virtue of what zoologists call "reciprocal altruism". I think this sense of struggle that we can see in the world, the continual struggle to achieve peace in the face of violence, is the struggle that we all have in our individual lives, and that our patients bring us. They are striving to be good, to live well, to lead a better life, and for reasons they do not understand they cannot do that. In Kleinian language they want to move from the paranoid–schizoid position to the depressive position; from a way of living that is dominated by impulse and therefore essentially unfree, to a way of living that is freer, involving relationship, the capacity to symbolize, and what Buddhists would call "mindfulness". My final point is to defend the word spiritual in its traditional sense. If we take a Platonic approach, that there is an Ultimate Reality that we can never know but, in a sense, strive to become, then anything to do with that striving can be termed "spiritual", not just to contrast it with the "material", but to emphasize by usage and tradition, something truer, nobler, higher, the absolute, the good.

References

Bion, W. R. (1965). *Transformations*. London: Heinemann

Clough, A. H. (1862)[1996]. The latest decalogue. In: Angela Partington (Ed.), *Oxford Dictionary of Quotations*. Oxford: Oxford University Press.

Coleridge, S. T. (1802)[1959]. Dejection: A letter. In: James Reeves (Ed.), *Selected Poems of Samuel Taylor Coleridge*. London. Heinemann.

Darwin, C. (1859). *On the Origin of Species*. London: John Murray.

Jung, C. G. (1963). *Memories, Dreams, Reflections*. London: Routledge [reprinted Collins, 1959].

Jung, C. G.(1971). *Psychological Types*, C.W., 6. London. Routledge.

Winnicott, D. W. (1965). The theory of the parent–infant relationship. In: *The Maturational Processes and the Facilitating Environment*. London: Hogarth.

Wordsworth, W. (1799)[1985]. The prelude. In: J. Wordsworth (Ed.), *The Two-Part Prelude*. Cambridge. Cambridge University Press.

Have "objects" got faces?

Kenneth Wright

"Let them not make me a stone. . . .
Otherwise kill me"

Louis MacNeice, "Prayer before Birth"

Introduction

I t is just a hundred years since William James (1902) delivered his famous Gifford Lectures on *The Varieties of Religious Experience* and almost fifty since I stumbled upon them and was bowled over. I had never before known that the world of religion in which I had grown up could be viewed so dispassionately, yet sympathetically. I had been trapped in the confines of a dogmatic world view and James appeared as my liberator. His thoughtful overview of the world I inhabited was entirely opportune and without hesitation I granted him "great man" status in my personal academy.

James' lectures were breathtaking in perspective and erudition. By contrast, I shall start from my own small corner of the universe. For not only would I find it hard to offer a Jamesian overview; I also

41

think that a personal and autobiographical approach has strengths of its own. Spirituality is subjective by its very nature, and the fact that it involves solitude and communion with one's own self gives further grounds for taking one's own experience as a starting point.

Autobiography

My own childhood was spent in a very religious household and, from the beginning, righteousness was pressed on me in restrictive and often frightening ways. "Thou shalt!" and "Thou shalt not!" were its governing precepts and I remember at the age of ten my father, not normally a violent man, threatening to thrash me if I did not go to church with him. In this authoritarian and imposed religious environment, three things were important: *dogma*, which meant having to believe the right things; *conformity*, which meant having to obey the right rules; and *sin*, which meant the inevitability of transgressing those rules and the ever present risk of hell-fire and damnation. My childhood religion was thus far from being life supportive—a claim it sometimes made. And it did not help to achieve inner security (another of its claims), unless one preferred *eternal* life to life in this world. On the contrary, it undermined security with excessive guilt and cramped attempts at living with debilitating fear. Although no doubt intended to guide one to a better life, its true effects on the psyche were crushing. For me, at least, it engendered a need to escape from religion because any attempt to live life fully, as a real person in my own body, was branded in advance as sinful.

It is scarcely surprising that as I moved into adolescence my antipathy towards religion grew apace. I wanted to break free but held back from the isolation and guilt such a break would entail. Needless to say, my teenage years were far from typical. While my peers experimented enthusiastically with their own bodies and the opposite sex, I cultivated solitude as I read and sweated my way out of religious belief. It took many years to extricate myself, and not until my twenties did I begin to feel intellectually free.

On a feeling level, things were more complicated: my newly found freedom could easily be undermined by nostalgia for the old religion. And even after the "death of god", something always remained that I now wish to examine. I am not referring to the guilt that persisted at having destroyed in myself the beliefs my parents held dear, but to something more positive that had been overshadowed by the imposed religious practices of my childhood.

In his Gifford Lectures, William James had made a distinction between institutional and personal religion and when I look back, it was clearly institutional religion from which I suffered. It was institutional religion that limited my world, and institutional religion I finally turned my back on. I think that all along, however, I was aware of another and different strand. This did not consist in what I had been taught—in what had been inculcated into me—but in something more spontaneous, perhaps even innate. I now think of this as a sensibility towards the natural world that I had discovered in myself from quite an early age and somehow managed to protect from institutional and parental pressures. I refer to the fact that for as long as I can remember the natural world affected me powerfully, evoking experiences that seemed intensely significant. I think that alongside the religion I was taught I became a nature worshipper.

Perhaps I was a kind of nature mystic engaged in a solitary and intuitive practice? For as a lonely child, wandering the lanes and fields around my home, I gave myself up to the sensual forms of the natural world that surrounded me. Had I been asked, as children often are, what I wanted to be when I grew up, I would have replied without hesitation: "a naturalist", for that is what I felt myself to be. I had no notion at that time of being a biologist or natural scientist. To me "being a naturalist" meant one thing only: that I could remain in communion with nature for the rest of my life. For this, more than anything else, and certainly more than the religion I was force-fed, was the nurturing that kept me alive. With analytic hindsight, I would say that I was living in a state of what Jung (1933) termed *participation mystique*, and Michael Balint (1959), in the context of mother and baby interaction, *harmonious interpenetrating mix-up*. This was a good state and I did not want to give it up.

It may seem odd to say that my bicycle was part of this happy state of affairs. Although just after the war a bike was still an important means of getting about, to me it was more than this, and like the natural world seemed almost an extension of me. In the same way that nature seemed to *embody* and *look after* a core of disallowed feelings, so my bike *embodied* and *looked after* my joy in physical mastery. In an unreflective way, I had found a means of looking after myself, of cherishing those parts of my self that felt unloved and unrecognized. In communing with nature, and giving myself over to the rhythms of riding my bike, I had found a way of preserving myself from the clutches of well-meaning mentors.

Words and music

As a child I could not have put any of this into words. But, as I started to read more widely, I sometimes would come upon an author towards whom I felt a particular resonance. Such an author seemed to speak to me of something I had always known, articulating experiences that were part of me but as yet dimly realized. At first I made such discoveries through poetry: Wordsworth, with his untrammelled worship of nature and Gerard Manly Hopkins, for whom nature and the Christian God were more closely intertwined. But then there was Rousseau, a poet in spirit if not in fact, who stirred me with his romantic *Confessions* (Rousseau, 1770). And there were many others: from adolescence on, I collected and treasured a compendium of lines and phrases that spoke to my deepest feelings. Although nothing was planned or ordered, the lines would engrave themselves in my mind so that I created, in Yeats' words, a "rag and bone shop of the heart" (Yeats, 1994).

Later, music played a vital role, even though the only available sources were my grandfather's wind-up gramophone, a "wireless", as it was then called, and the hymns we sang in church. The wireless in those days was quite a public thing—strictly one per house and no earphones. But I can remember gluing myself to it, twiddling the knob for hours on end, trying to catch whatever I could from classical concerts or hilly-billy songs. What were these beautiful snippets, these wonderful sounds? O brave new world that hath such forms in it!

It must have been important that I could share these musical discoveries with my mother, and that she too valued them, perhaps also finding in the music a confirming echo of her unsung self. Be that as it may, I now shared with her my newly discovered snippets of music, just as previously I had brought back to her the things I had collected on my wanderings: the flowers I had picked, the plants I had dug up, the interesting stones I had found. Being able to share these things created a sense of mutual discovery and enjoyment.

When I now try and make sense of this, I think that somehow I had discovered *a spiritual recipe*—a formula for taking care of my inner self. The process I had stumbled upon had a number of elements, above all a capacity *to be receptive* to things, *to feel a connection* with them. It also involved a sense of *communication* between things "out there"—be it nature, poetry, or music—and a part of myself that I scarcely knew. The process was not something I could do at will, but when it worked, there was a *resonance*, or "hit", as though something "out there" had *spoken to* some feeling "in here" and *recognized* it. I have called this an experience of "deep calling unto deep" (Wright, 1998). Such experiences may sometimes be shared but the sense of their validity is essentially subjective. I *knew*, for example, that my nature experiences sustained me, and that was that.

I referred earlier to Yeats's "rag and bone shop of the heart" as the place where such experiences are collected: "I must lie down where all the ladders start / in the foul rag and bone shop of the heart". But my "rag and bone shop" was OK, in spite of the fact that my religion regarded much in the human heart as "foul". For it was a sanctuary of rescued bits and pieces in which erstwhile "foul" feelings had been brought into the human fold. It was a place in which elements of raw emotion had found a place to be, a containing place where "all is safely gathered in . . ." as the hymn so nicely puts it. What gathered emotion into this containing place was the repertoire of resonating forms, and in the circumstances I am describing, these were the forms of art and nature, not, as would often be the case, forms mediated to the child by the mother. In this sense a person's collection of forms, their rag and bone shop of *objets trouvés*, is compensatory to maternal failure. But the fact that it works, that the resonating landscape, the bit of music, the fragment of poetry "take care" of the self, and "look after it"—this was something I learned, or thought I did, as I struggled to stay afloat in the turbulent waters of adolescence. This idea has become important in my adult thinking, and I now regard it as pivotal to an understanding of the spiritual life.

Philosophy

This account of my own trajectory would not be complete if it failed to describe the potential importance of philosophical thought in tying together the delicate fabric of the self. As I moved into adolescence, my quest for validating forms became more intellectual and in pursuit of "salvation", as I sometimes thought of it, I often went to the public library, scanning and searching the philosophy section for help and inspiration. How did such scanning work? It worked through resonance, and in order to illustrate this I shall mention just a few of the books (and philosophers) I discovered.

One day I came upon Freud's "Introductory lectures" (Freud, 1916–1917). These made a powerful impact, especially the notion that sex, forbidden and proscribed in my own narrow world, lay at the centre of all human activity. In spite of this, I did not then know what to do with Freud and as a result we passed each other by. I made a mental note that he was big and important but there was no resonance with anything inside. During the same period, I discovered James' lectures on religious experience (James, 1902) with which I started this paper. Again the sense of big ideas, but on this occasion, there was something else—the sense of being "addressed" and "spoken to". This was not just because James was talking about religion, though clearly that was important. There was a direct appeal, missing for me in Freud at that time. When Freud "spoke", I may have wondered, with a kind of intellectual curiosity, what manner of psychopathology mine might be? But when James "spoke", the accord was immediate: I had no doubt that I was a "divided self" who needed to be "twice born" in order to be happy. Finally, while James seemed to give me permission to feel the way I did, making it all right in a human kind of way, Freud made me feel small and immature. In so far as I saw myself in the pages of his text, I felt I was a "case" or "specimen", and this was not the help I needed.

My intellectual quest led me to two other writers, both of whom influenced me profoundly. One was Carl Jung, the other the Jewish philosopher Martin Buber. Both writers had for me the quality of resonance and both seemed to "speak to my condition". When, for example, I picked up Jung's *Modern Man in Search of a Soul* (Jung, 1933), I immediately felt: "Yes! That's me!" And when I read the opening lines of Buber's *I and Thou* (Buber, 1937), I again felt the same shiver of excitement.

I read as much of Jung as I could find and remember thinking he was the one person in the world who could help me. I thought of going to Zurich, but of course that never happened: I was twenty, a medical student, and utterly impoverished. I regret that I never had a Jungian analysis but at the same time there was something about Jung that frightened me. His gaze was exclusively inward, and perhaps I feared losing contact with reality if I followed him. Even then I realized that I needed to be less solipsistic and to risk more encounter with the world.

And encounter was precisely what my other *guru* Martin Buber seemed to promise: "In the beginning is relation" (1937, p. 18). Buber beckoned me out of my shell. *I and Thou*, a mere 120 pages of philosophical and poetic utterances, spoke to my heart as well as my head. As a rabbi, his intention was to touch and change the reader: "All real living is meeting". (1937, p. 11). To me, at that time, he seemed to be saying: "Stop going round inside yourself, and step out to the encounter that will change you! Allow yourself to be touched!" Unlike Jung, he pointed outwards; salvation lay in something out there, not in deeper immersion in one's own self. Such an encounter might be difficult to define precisely, but Buber managed to stir something important in me.

For Buber, a certain kind of relatedness to the external world is central to both human life and spirituality: *I–Thou*—the primary word spoken with the whole being: "In the beginning is relation". Not to oneself, not to one's own psyche, but to this Other, unique and present, filling my world. The transforming glimpse is of grace, being, and truth, but fated to fade away, to fall back into something more manageable and ordered, prosaic and describable: *I–It*, the Other as object.

I–Thou, I–It—these forms of relation alternate and give way to one another, the *Thou* giving meaning and point to life, the *It* order and stability. Each is a counterpoint to the other, but while the *Thou* is intrinsically evanescent, the *It* is solid and permanent, the very fabric of our lives. "Without *It* man cannot live. But he who lives with *It* alone is not a man (Buber, 1937, p. 34)." "You cannot hold onto life without it, its reliability sustains you; but should you die in it your grave would be in nothingness" (*ibid.*, p. 32). The *Thou* opens the door to the spiritual, and for Buber the spiritual is rooted in relation.

Recapitulation: towards a definition of the spiritual.

I shall now pull together what I have said and see if it is possible to discern within it an embryonic theory of spirituality. In talking of my own experience, I concluded that the spiritual seemed to involve something that in colloquial terms "validated", "contained", and "looked after" the self. It involved a feeling of recognition of the experiential self by something or someone that existed outside of it. This did not have to be another human being but could be something as simple as the contours and textures of a landscape, a line of poetry or a phrase of music. This validating process did not have to involve knowledge or understanding but was more immediate and felt. The music, the line of poetry, the natural form, echoed or resonated *directly* with the shape, timbre and rhythm of the inner feeling. It could be said, following Langer (1942, 1953), that such a resonating form is a particular kind of symbol; it has the capacity to *recreate* that which it represents, not merely to point to it, or refer to it. A symbol of this kind *reproduces* the shape or sentience of an actual feeling and this is made possible by the structure of the symbol. Unlike words that are referential, such symbols are homologous, or isomorphic with that which they represent. For this reason, Langer called them *presentational* symbols, because they *present* experience rather than merely referring to it. The tree or landscape allows itself to be transformed into a containing symbol of feeling. And according to Winnicott, this is the way the baby's transitional object works—the bit of blanket allows itself to be made into a concrete symbol of maternal experience. It is the homologous form of the symbol—its *presentational* quality—that enables it to preserve the element of experience and recreate it when it is needed.

In my own case, the discovery of such a means of safeguarding experience was crucial in limiting the damage from a doctrinaire religious upbringing. It helped me to hold off the destructive impact of dogmatic assaults and to keep my own way of feeling going within the rag and bone shop of my heart.

There is a poem by Louis MacNeice that illustrates some aspects of the process I am talking about. In its content, the poem emphasizes all the dangerous and negative elements that conspire against the life of the self, that collectively Winnicott would have called *impingements* (Winnicott, 1965). On the other hand, in its structure and rhythm, its melodic line, it provides precisely that structure that the poet needs to "look after" and preserve the self from such threats. The poem takes the form of a prayer and is called "Prayer before Birth".

> I am not yet born; O hear me.
> Let not the bloodsucking bat or the rat or the stoat or the
>   club-footed ghoul come near me.
>
> I am not yet born, console me.
> I fear that the human race may with tall walls wall me,
>   with strong drugs dope me, with wise lies lure me,
>   on black racks rack me, in blood baths roll me.
>   [MacNeice, 1964, p. 74]

These two verses, and indeed the whole poem, evoke the spectre of being destroyed as a live and feeling self. But the next verse evokes beneficent and loving images of that which will look after the self and protect it from the insults and injuries of which the poet is afraid. The images in this verse are maternal, but couched in terms of the natural world. They relate closely to that provision of forms by the natural world I have previously discussed.

> I am not yet born; provide me
> With water to dandle me, grass to grow for me, trees to talk
>   to me, sky to sing to me, birds and a white light
>   in the back of my mind to guide me.
>   [*ibid.*]

These images are invoked to maintain and safeguard the continuity of the poet's inner experience. There follow two more verses, then a last verse which brings back an even more terrifying catalogue of assaults and threats to the poet's self, and of course, a prayer to "someone" to preserve him from them:

I am not yet born; O fill me
With strength against those who would freeze my
  humanity, would dragoon me into a lethal automoton,
    would make me a cog in a machine, a thing with
      one face, a thing, and against all those
        who would dissipate my entirety, would
          blow me like thistledown hither and
            thither or hither and thither
              like water held in the
                hands would spill me.

Let them not make me a stone and let them not spill me.
Otherwise kill me.

[*ibid.*]

"Let them not make me a stone . . . / Otherwise kill me". It is better to be literally dead than suffer the *living* death which being turned into a stone implies. These images remind me of the Medusa myth, in which the stare of the hag-like Gorgon turns the beholder into stone. It is the objectification of the subject the poet fears, the relegation to a thing-like status. *I–Thou* becomes *I–It;* I become nothing but your object.

Towards a definition of the spiritual

I started my paper with the hope of reaching a working definition of the spiritual. *I shall now assert that the spiritual is anything that contributes to keeping our humanity alive. It is anything that helps us to stay in touch with the life of the self and anything that enriches that life. It is also anything that safeguards the self against the dangers of dissolution or petrification, of being transformed into the Other's object or thing.*

I am aware that this is a broad and general definition. Nevertheless, it does have some advantages. It completely eschews metaphysics and in that sense is firmly grounded within the everyday world. It invokes no outside agencies such as god, and refers to an area of psychological functioning of potential concern to everybody. It allows us to consider how spiritual inputs might work within the psychic economy. And it allows us to think developmentally in terms of the origin and growth of such concerns. It is not overly moral or concerned with wrongdoing and guilt. And finally, it is not incompatible with the broad sweep of many spiritual disciplines that generally purport to lead a person towards enrichment of their personal life in non-material ways. I am not suggesting that my definition is comprehensive—I am not, in Jamesian fashion, surveying the entire field of the spiritual. I am, however, proposing that one root of the spiritual may lie in a type of maternal response that first occurs in infancy. It is to this developmental aspect that I now turn.

Developmental considerations

In the last part of my paper, I want to think developmentally: "What are the roots of spirituality in early life?" I shall also raise some questions about psychological theories, asking if they give enough weight to the spiritual in the way they are formulated. And finally I shall reflect on artistic activity and consider if there is any relation between this and spirituality.

In an earlier publication (Wright, 1991) I have written about the role of the mother's face in the early development of the self. I have expressed dissatisfaction with psychoanalytic theories that place the body and bodily satisfaction at the centre of everything, and have argued that psychoanalytic theory lacks a proper place for the human face, leading to an imbalance in its thinking.

I shall now make two assertions. Firstly, that the face—more specifically, the infant's relation to the mother's face—lies at the root of the spiritual in human beings. And secondly, that because the face is left out of psychoanalytic theory, the spiritual is hard pressed to find a place there.

These are broad claims, but more recently there have been developments in which the face, implicitly or explicitly, begins to have greater importance. In England, the later Winnicott is a prime example: I would note particularly his seminal paper in which he explored the mirror role of the mother's face for the infant's developing sense of self ("Mirror role of mother and family in child development", 1971a). A further example is Bowlby's attachment theory (1969)—largely ignored by mainstream psychoanalysis—which gives prominence to the smiling response in the growth of the infant's *attachment*. A very early, and again largely ignored precursor of Bowlby's attachment concept, was Ian Suttie's (1935) notion of a *primary need for the mother* independent of nurturing. It is interesting in this regard that Suttie was concerned with what Freud had left out of his theories, in particular, a credible account of human tenderness, and any sympathetic understanding of religion.

The above approaches have one thing in common: the idea that there are aspects of early relating, *independent of feeding and bodily satisfaction*, that have a fundamental role in infant development. Such views propose a *primary relational core* in human beings that is there from the beginning. It is not dependent on other experiences with the mother, but constitutes a primary inborn need for relational experience. Such a way of thinking begins to link up with Buber's tracing of the spiritual to an "inborn *Thou*": "In the beginning is relation".

These ideas are important because they point to an area of development in which the seeds of the spiritual might be found. Anaclitic developmental theories are *inherently materialistic*: we love our mothers only *because* they feed us. They are also relatively *unspecific*: if feeding is what gives rise to love, *there is nothing essentially specific and personal* at the heart of human loving. Finally, they downgrade infant–mother *communication* in shaping development and thus ignore what many would regard as the defining characteristic of human beings—the *richness of their communication* with each other.

In my own attempt to define the spiritual, these characteristics are precisely the ones that are important. That which is felt to be spiritual is *non-materialistic*—it does not involve material exchange. Second, it is bound up with a type of *communication and relational experience* mediated by preverbal symbols. And finally, this communication is *highly specific*: it involves a close fit between external form and inner experience, and its resonance and significance for the self depend on this.

Psychoanalytic theory developed in a nineteenth century scientific and materialistic culture and Freud was at pains to make his theories scientifically respectable. He had a jaundiced view of religion and would have been devastated to find that his theories had an affinity with it. His view of psychoanalysis as a science rooted in biology persisted through much of the twentieth century and still fights, albeit a losing battle, with more hermeneutic interpretations of the discipline. All this has perpetuated the materialistic bias of theory with which the anaclitic thesis sits so comfortably. However, in the past thirty years or so, psychoanalytic developmental theory has come under pressure from more empirically based infant research. A good summary can be found in Stern (1985). Such research has generated sharply divergent views of infant development, and these have begun to infiltrate, albeit slowly, some areas of the psychoanalytic establishment.

What these findings draw attention to is the richness of mother-infant communication from the beginning. They point to an infant for whom the *specificity* of the mother's response is significant from birth. And they demonstrate that *interfacial* communication is where it all happens. These findings give the face an equal claim to the breast as an early locus of formative transactions.

The good maternal face

This poses a challenge to traditional theory that, especially in the Kleinian school, places the breast (or experience at the breast), at the core of the infant's internal world. If, however, the face and preverbal communication of affect between mother and baby are now given the importance that infant research suggests, the case can also be made for *a good maternal face* at the core of the healthy personality.

This idea is important for my view of spirituality because the mother's face is the first *non-material* object in the baby's experience, and spirituality, as I understand it, is mediated through a non-material, i.e., symbolic relationship. In describing the face as a non-material object, I refer to the fact that the face as "face"—both as prime *gestalt* by which the mother is recognized, and as focus and locus of her expressiveness—can only be apprehended by the infant *from a distance and visually*. Although it can be, and often is, touched and grasped, it cannot in its essence be apprehended and possessed in the way that other objects can. What it *specifically* yields—*the changing patterns of emotional expression*—can *only* be grasped visually, i.e., non-materially.

This leads on to the question of what it might mean to say that an infant has internalized *a good maternal face*. What might a good maternal face provide?

In attempting to answer this, I shall begin with the Winnicott paper already referred to (Winnicott, 1971a). In it Winnicott asserts that the mother's face is the infant's first mirror. By this, he means that when the infant looks in the mother's face, what he sees there, in the mother's response, is a visible emotional reflection of his own self. It is not until much later, says Winnicott, when there is a keener sense of the mother's existence as a separate person, that the infant will see in her face a reflection of her mood. Winnicott suggests that in this moment of mirroring, the baby has a heightened sense of aliveness. If the mother's response truly reflects the baby's feeling state, it offers the baby a congruent and external form (her facial expression) through which to apprehend it.

There is a bridge here to my earlier discussion of the part played by resonating forms in the economy of the self. The form from nature, the snippet of music, the fragment of poetry—each confirms, and in some sense makes more real, the feeling with which it resonates. It could be said that it gives the feeling a form by which it can be apprehended and recalled; alternatively, that it provides a symbolic apprehension of something not previously noted, or incompletely realized. But, in each case, the net result is a feeling of emotional enhancement. "I feel more *me* because you have shared in, and responded to, my being alive in *specific* ways (mediated by a specific form) that show me you are in touch with what I am feeling." I have personalized the experience of resonance because I believe that is how it is often experienced.

It can be seen, then, that the mother's facial expressions fall into my general category of resonating responses. And as Winnicott points out, if the mother is unable to respond, because she is depressed, or for some other reason, there will be a baby, and perhaps later an adult, who feels less alive, less contained, and less secure. *There is no responsive internalized maternal face to look after the baby self.* Winnicott's paper thus begins to answer the question as to what a good maternal face provides: a repertoire of attuned emotional responses that mirror, and symbolically contain, in a primitive way, aspects of infant experience.

Attunement

Mirroring *facial* interactions of this kind are at their height during the first few months, perhaps the first year of life. As the baby gets older, during the second year, the repertoire of maternal responses widens. This has been eloquently described by Daniel Stern in his book *The Interpersonal World of the Infant* in the chapter on attunement (Stern, 1985). Stern defines an attunement as "a recasting . . . of an affective state" (p. 161), originally, the recasting by the *mother* of the *baby's* affective state. By *affective state*, he has in mind not so much the major emotions of joy, anger, disgust, and so on, but the less dramatic, and constantly changing, levels of arousal, interest, frustration, and satisfaction that accompany whatever the baby is doing. These lesser emotions, that Stern calls *vitality affects*, could be thought of as constituting the *emotional* fabric of the baby's life. Observation suggests that the mother more or less continually and subliminally attunes to these states and spontaneously enacts responses to them. These responses track and reproduce in an ongoing way the form of the infant's arousal. Thus, the mother may make a series of sounds with different rhythms and intensities; or she may move her body in rhythmical or other expressive ways. But in each case, the rhythm and "shape" of what the mother does will be isomorphic with what she has just witnessed in her baby. In this context, what is important is the fact that the mother's response constitutes a resonating *reflection*, or *portrayal*, of what the baby has just been feeling.

These attunement responses can be seen to be in continuity with the earlier facial mirroring described by Winnicott. And as in that case, it can be argued that the mother's response provides an iconic and fitting form that resonates with the feeling the infant has just enacted. Under the general heading of the "good maternal face", we can thus include the later repertoire of maternal responses. Even more cogently than with facial expressions, it can be argued that such visible maternal responses constitute, at least potentially, the material from which the baby might later construct representations and containers of its own experience.

It can now be seen that the resonating forms I spoke of at the beginning of my paper have a close affinity with the forms first provided by the attuned mother. Although now self-generated from the wider environment, whether the world of art and culture or the world of nature, they perpetuate a maternal function of safeguarding and looking after the self.

This is the ground for my claim that the roots of the spiritual lie in infancy. The processes we deem spiritual in their effect form a continuous line with the resonating responses that supported and contained our early experiences of liveliness. In a recent paper on artistic creativity (Wright, 1998), I spoke of such responses as "making experience sing." I believe that in the good enough situation, they do not merely preserve experience from destruction but actually enhance and confirm it.

Singing masters of the soul

I shall conclude with some comments on a poem by W. B. Yeats that can be seen as illustrating what I have said about maternal attunement. Perhaps it merely provides a text on which to string my thoughts, but the childhood experience of sitting through countless sermons taught me this, if nothing else, that a text makes a wonderful starting point for almost anywhere you want to go! The poem I shall discuss is "Sailing to Byzantium" (Yeats, 1994).

"That is no country for old men . . ." exclaims the poet. Why? Because all around is creation and procreation: "The young / in one another's arms. . . / the salmon-falls, the mackerel-crowded seas . . ." He feels surrounded by too much immediacy and sensuality—for an old man, at any rate. He takes a step back and sees that something is left out, a spiritual creativity that might redeem the decay of old age: "Caught in that sensual music all neglect / Monuments of unageing intellect", And then he reflects on the predicament of getting old:

> An aged man is but a paltry thing,
> A tattered coat upon a stick, unless
> Soul clap its hands and sing, and louder sing
> For every tatter in its mortal dress,
> Nor is there singing school but studying
> Monuments of its own magnificence . . .

The relevant idea is this: that soul must "clap its hands and sing, and louder sing" to cope with the ebbing away of old age and the threat of dissolution. Yeats's answer to this threat is to go to Byzantium, which for him is a kind of Mecca of the soul. Byzantium is a repository of the spiritual and there he will find in abundance monuments to the soul's magnificence:

> And therefore I have sailed the seas and come
> To the holy city of Byzantium.

He then invokes, with something like a prayer, the sages portrayed in the gold mosaics:

> O sages standing in God's holy fire
> As in the gold mosaic of a wall,
> Come from the holy fire, perne in a gyre,
> And be the singing-masters of my soul . . .

"Come from the holy fire . . . and be the singing masters of my soul.". His soul is in desperate need of a singing master if it is to survive. On the surface, this is because old age is taking its toll on his physical and sensual capacities. But I think one can also sense here a fear of impending disintegration, something more like Bion's "nameless dread" or Winnicott's "unthinkable anxieties". The loss of self, the loss of a *sense* of being alive—these can afflict a person at any time of their life.

I would suggest that this more universal kind of anxiety can be seen in another of Yeats' poems, "The Second Coming" (Yeats, 1994). Here, too, he writes of an impending chaos, presaged in the following lines:

> Turning and turning in a widening gyre
> The falcon cannot hear the falconer . . .

In this image there is loss of an essential contact—the falcon losing contact with the falconer just as the baby may lose contact with the responding mother. And then there are consequences:

> Things fall apart; the centre cannot hold;
> Mere anarchy is loosed upon the world,

> The blood-dimmed tide is loosed, and everywhere
> The ceremony of innocence is drowned . . .

These dire events can be seen as an echo of what may happen in the baby when the baby loses touch with the responding mother. The sense of being begins to fall apart, and the need for rescue or salvation becomes pressing. Yeats reaches out for the "singing masters of the soul", the "sages standing in God's holy fire . . ." But to whom can the baby reach out?

The baby, of course, reaches out to the mother, and at different times for different elements of what she is able to provide. It may be her breast, but in this paper I have focused on certain *non-material* elements in her repertoire of responses—her facial expressions and her responsive "songs". I have sought to understand the significance and importance of these for the developing infant, and I have, in effect, suggested that the mother is the first singing master of the infant's soul. If she stops singing and responding, the infant is in danger of disintegrating. If her mirroring face and attuned responses have been good enough, the infant will internalize that maternal face sufficiently to be able to hold on to it in times of need. The mother will go on singing inside the child's mind (Wright, 2000). But if the mother is too long away—a situation that Winnicott often spoke about (e.g., 1967b)—everything is thrown into disarray: "Things fall apart / the centre cannot hold . . .". What happens in the face of this impending crisis depends on the answer to another question: has the child been able to internalize, not merely a repertoire of remembered maternal responses that will surely help, but the mother's song-making function itself?

To say that the child has internalized the mother's function means, I think, that the child (or later the adult) is not restricted to a limited repertoire of responses—in this case, the mother's actual "songs". Instead, there is a capacity to generate one's own forms or songs, with similar purpose and effect. Such a person, it might be said, is now capable of looking after his own spiritual well-being.

How and why some individuals can achieve such an internalization and others not is an intriguing question. Perhaps in some degree it is the norm in a good enough situation—a part of the capacity to be creative. Certain individuals, however, among them creative artists, seem to develop this capacity to an extraordinary degree. As Yeats saw, and invoked in his poem, the creative artist is not only a singing master of his own soul but plays this part for any who wish to hear.

In my view, the psychotherapist is also a kind of artist, and also in his way tries to be a singing master of the soul. The provision of resonating forms is an essential part of his stock in trade, but I shall finish with a teasing thought: that just as there are no firm criteria for distinguishing a good artist from a bad one, so are there no certain ways of distinguishing a good psychotherapist. When it comes to spiritual matters the judgement is always subjective, and the ultimate arbiter of "rightness" is the individual heart.

References

Balint, M. (1959). *Thrills and Regressions.* London: Hogarth Press.

Bowlby, J. (1969). *Attachment and Loss,* vol 1, *Attachment.* London: Hogarth Press.

Buber, M. (1937). *I and Thou,* R, Gregor Smith, Trans.). Edinburgh: Clark.

Freud, S. (1916–1917). Introductory lectures on psychoanalysis. *S.E.,* *15–16.* London. Hogarth Press

James, W. (1902). *The Varieties of Religious Experience.* London: Longmans Green.

Jung, C. G. (1933). *Modern Man in Search of a Soul.* New York: Harvest.

Langer, S. K. (1942). *Philosophy in a New Key.* Cambridge, MA: Harvard University Press.

Langer, S. K. (1953). *Feeling and Form.* London: Routledge and Kegan Paul.

MacNeice, L. (1964). *Selected Poems of Louis MacNeice,* W. H. Auden (Ed.). London: Faber and Faber.

Rousseau, J.-J. (1770)[2000]. *Confessions.* P. Coleman (Ed.). Oxford: Oxford University Press.

Stern, D. (1985). *The Interpersonal World of the Infant.* New York: Basic Books.

Suttie, I. D. (1935). *The Origins of Love and Hate.* London: Kegan Paul.

Winnicott, D. W. (1965). Ego integration in child development. In: *The Maturational Processes and the Facilitating Environment.* London: Hogarth Press.

Winnicott, D.W. (1971a) Mirror role of mother and family in child development. In: *Playing and Reality*. London: Tavistock.
Winnicott, D. W. (1971b). The location of cultural experience. In: *Playing and Reality*. London: Tavistock.
Wright, K. (1991). *Vision and Separation: Between Mother and Baby*. London: Free Association Books.
Wright, K. (1998). Deep calling unto deep: artistic creativity and the maternal object. *British Journal of Psychotherapy, 14*, 453–467.
Wright, K. (2000). To make experience sing. In: L. Caldwell (Ed.), *Art, Creativity, Living*. London: Karnac.
Yeats, W. B. (1994). *The Collected Poems of W. B. Yeats*. Ware Wordsworth Editions.

RESPONSE BY TOM MCDONNELL

I hope that I can make a resonant response to Kenneth Wright's evocative and poetic paper with its strongly autobiographical flavour. I was often put in mind of the young Wordsworth of "The Prelude", as the boy Ken rode down country lanes on his beloved bike, picking flowers for his mother, or at home, offering her musical tit-bits, as he began experiencing the growth of his creative sensibility.

I am very much in sympathy with the central tenets of this paper. I, too, feel that the mother's face, and indeed the total experience at the breast are at the roots of our spiritual and creative life. I also feel that the consequences of failure of this primary interaction are potentially damaging. The Medusa-like gaze of a mother can, as it were, turn the infant's mind to stone, whether that look comes from within mother, or is projected into her by the infant as an interpretation of the absence he sees in her face. This can lead to other petrifications in later life when, trying to deal with the hostile gaze, or indeed the hostile regard or hostile view of the other, we become paralysed, impotent. We can also feel overwhelming shame in the face of the other's objectifying or accusing gaze, when it meets with not enough selfhood nor enough sense of capacity to restore or repair. We lower our eyes to avoid being seen, or to avoid seeing that we are being seen in our exposed state. It is often because of "loss of face" that we become involved in road-rage incidents and, more tragically, choose to go to war.

Given my sympathy with the paper, what then is my chosen task? I noticed how often the word "resonant" appeared in this paper. The *Shorter Oxford* defines "resonant" as "continuing to sound, or ring, re-echoing and resounding". Ken Wright's paper certainly set me thinking and feeling, and it continues to sound and re-echo in my mind and in my clinical work.

A patient who came to me some years ago said, at the end of his assessment session, that he feared there would be no room for the spiritual in his proposed therapy with me. I asked him why he thought that, and he said that he imagined that he would become a Freudian specimen in my jar, that the experience would be dry and emotionless, and that notions of good and bad would be largely irrelevant. We finished five years later with his personal god still intact and my sense of the good object still holding its place firmly in the therapy. A lot of valuable work did take place in his use of fragments from the Old and New Testaments. They seemed to fit in very naturally with the general flow of our work together.

Religion, at least, the institutionalized variety, does not come off well in Ken Wright's paper. He experienced it as stifling, negative, and non-life-enhancing, so that in his childhood a growing sensibility to nature offered him a bulwark against the harsh superegoish depredations of religion. It seemed that religion was actually destroying the self. I was very moved by Dr Wright's use of Yeats's "rag and bone shop of the heart" as he battled for connections with his inner self. Feeling impoverished, he scoured his environment for bits and pieces of nourishment—Wordsworth, Hopkins, Buber, Freud, Jung, Rousseau, and, of course, music—a magpie struggling to build a spiritual nest. A wonderful diet. Having read *Les Rêveries Du Promeneur Solitaire* who could ever forget Rousseau's experience (what he called "le sentiment de l'existence") on Lake Geneva, when, having put down the oars of his boat, he lay on his back, drifting aimlessly, gazing up at an immense cloudless sky, and suddenly apprehended that everything made sense, and for those few seconds seemed to understand the meaning of being alive (Rousseau, 1960). I think we have all had such moments, and they do seem to have a connection with Michael Balint's concept of the "harmonious interpenetrating mix-up", between mother and infant (Balint, 1968). Wright quotes from Louis MacNeice's poem "Prayer before Birth", "Let them not make me a stone, and let them not spill me / Otherwise kill me" (Wright, 2003).

I often meet patients who have, in one way or another, "been turned to stone". This seems to me to be an extremely creative way to think about "stuckness" in a patient who, for example, has been petrified by his fear of failure, or even success; perhaps a young office-worker who has been so hounded by a persecutory boss, and has gone into such a desperate place of identification with the aggressor, that no real thought about his situation is possible. Such individuals have become so frozen with terror at the possibility of any form of emotional closeness that their lives are lived in isolation and persecution. Often a long and pain-filled therapy is the only way out of such despair and desolation.

I noticed that Dr Wright did not make specific mention of an internal Medusa: a way of describing an internalized version of early experience that has vitiated the self. The internal gorgon, in order to defend primitive omnipotence, lives in the projective mode, endlessly projecting into others and into parts of the self in order to control experience. One could say for our purposes that the mission of this internalized Medusa is death of the spiritual, the creative, and of reality—all deadly enemies of the phantasy of omnipotence.

I want to stay for a moment with the myth of Perseus as he confronts the deadly Medusa-gorgon. The goddess Athene steps in and advises Perseus not to look directly at Medusa, but to look at her through the reflection of the shield. Wright sees it as a shield of resonant and holding reflections. I thought, similarly, of Bion's alpha function, but was reminded also of what Neville Symington said to a patient, "If you've got me here beside you, looking with you, it just might be possible for you to look at this awful thing" (Symington, 1986, p. 325).

So how do we link spirituality and psychotherapy? For Ken Wright spirituality involves something that validates, contains, and "looks after" or "takes care of" the self in a particular way. It involves a feeling of recognition of the living parts of the self by something or someone that exists outside of the self. This validating experience does not necessarily involve knowledge or understanding, but something more immediate and felt. The music, the line of poetry, the natural form resonates directly with the shape, timbre, rhythm, and texture or the inner feeling. And surely this is exactly what psychotherapy does at its best. The therapist creates a place where the true self can be found. The therapist endeavours to provide an external environment where the internal world can be symbolized and permits the authentic self to be alive and to grow.

"In the beginning is relation" says Martin Buber "All true living is meeting" (cited in Wright, 2003). This is the other cornerstone of Dr Wright's paper. And of course, in the beginning is the mother's face. He would like to give the face at least an equal claim to the breast as a focus of foundational experiences. At this point I would like to enter the unique world of Donald Meltzer, as he is a theorist who has said a great deal about the importance of the mother's face and gaze. For Meltzer, the mother's face is above all an enigma to the newly born child. The baby is a passionate creature indeed, ripe and ready for an intense love affair with mother. Whom does he meet then? "The ordinary beautiful devoted mother presents to her ordinary beautiful baby, a complex object of overwhelming interest both sensual and infrasensual . . . But the meaning of his mother's behaviour, of the appearance and disappearance of the breast, and of the light in her eyes, of a face over which emotions pass like the shadows of clouds over the landscape, are unknown to him." (Meltzer, 1988, p. 22). Is mother all giving or all withholding? This is what Meltzer calls the aesthetic conflict, which he sees as the conflict between "the aesthetic impact of the outside of the 'beautiful' mother, available to the senses, and the enigmatic inside which can only be reached via creative imagination" (ibid.).

Meltzer feels that "Everything in art and literature, every analysis testifies to its perseverance through life" (ibid.). This is a view of the mother as La Giaconda. Tourists flock to the Louvre to gaze at that enigmatic smile . . . or is it a smile? Is the painting that good, that much better than the others, or does La Giaconda stir up primitive feelings in all of us as to whether we are truly loved or not. As children chant to each other as they pick the petals from flowers, "she loves me, she loves me not . . ."

The aesthetic conflict is not really defined by Meltzer. But he does tell us that the core of the aesthetic experience resides not in the transience of the object, as in the Romantic Agony, but in its enigmatic quality (Meltzer, 1988). The pain is that of deep uncertainty, distrust, and suspicion. Rescue from this conflict lies in the quest for knowledge, Bion's K link, the desire to know, rather than the desire to possess. The K link moves us away from a yearning for narcissistic gratification and control over the object. The desire to know demands that the object be given its freedom (Meltzer, 1988).

Winnicott also spoke of the enigma of the mother's face:

> Some babies . . . study the variable maternal visage in an attempt to predict the mother's mood, just exactly as we all study the weather The baby quickly learns to make a forecast. Just now it is safe to forget the mother's mood and to be spontaneous, but at any minute the mother's face will become fixed or her mood will dominate and my personal needs must then be withdrawn, otherwise my central self may suffer insult . . . If the mother's face is unresponsive, then a mirror is a thing to be looked at, but not be looked into. [Winnicott, 1971, p. 132]

What are the consequences of a mother seeing her child not as subject but as mother's object? This objectifying gaze, of the mother who demands compliance from her child and sees the child as a container for her own projections, can lead to petrification of the child's sense of self. On the other hand, when mother's mirroring gaze and attuned responses have been "good enough", the child will have taken in enough to feel contained and held, as the mother's mind resonates in the child's mind.

Dr Wright does not specifically mention the father, although we might think that he is always implicit in the paper. Naturally the father's face and eyes are part of primary experience too. However, the first encounter with the father (the "other" in relation to mother) depends greatly on the extent to which a secure maternal object has been internalized and established. This makes it possible for triangular space to exist, with its links between the three persons of the oedipal triangle. Thus we are given a capacity for seeing ourselves in interaction with others and for entertaining another point of view, while retaining our own; for reflecting on ourselves while being ourselves.

What happens when our patients use the couch, and we are not face to face with them? I was told a story recently by a therapist who had been seeing a patient for many, many years, three times a week on the couch. Nearing the end of the therapy, the patient decided she wanted to sit up and face the therapist for the concluding sessions. The therapist told me how shocked she was to see the patient as it were for the first time in a decade or more. Her patient had grown quite old. I find it a poignant account, and felt there was a significant loss involved. Had a certain amount of vital information been lost in seeing so little of the patient's face during those years?

In the beginning, in the middle, in the end also, is "relation", according to Martin Buber. As I have said very little about "I—thou" relationships, which are extremely important in Ken Wright's work and thinking, I thought I would finish my response to his resonant paper with a short poem by Donne.

The Good Morrow

> I Wonder by my troth, what thou, and I
> Did, till we lov'd? Were we not wean'd till then?
> But suck'd on countrey pleasures, childishly?
> Or snorted we in the seaven sleepers den?
> T'was so; But this, all pleasures fancies bee.
> If ever any beauty I did see,
> Which I desir'd, and got, t'was but a dreame of thee.
>
> And now good morrow to our waking soules.
> Which watch not one another out of feare;
> For love, all love of other sights controules
> And makes one little roome an every where.
> Let sea-discoverers to new worlds have gone,
> Let Maps to other, worlds on worlds have showne,
> Let us possesse one world, each hath one, and is one.
>
> My face in thine eye, thine in mine appeares,
> And true plaine hearts doe in the faces rest,
> Where can we finde two better hemispheares

Without sharpe North, without declining West?
What ever dyes, was not mixt equally;
If our two loves be one, or, thou and I
Love so alike, that none doe slacken, none can die.

[Donne, 1912]

References

Balint, M. (1968). *The Basic Fault*. London: Tavistock.

Donne, J. (1912). Songs and sonnets from 1635–1669. In: H. Grierson (Ed.), *Donne: Poetical Works*. London: Oxford University Press.

MacNeice, L. (1964). Prayer Before Birth. In: W. H. Auden (Ed.), *Selected Poems of Louis MacNeice*: London. Faber and Faber.

Meltzer, D. (1988). Aesthetic conflict: its place in development. In: D. Meltzer & M. Harris Williams, *The Apprehension of Beauty*. Strath Tay, Perthshire: Clunie Press.

Symington, N. (1986). *The Analytic Experience*. London: Free Association Books.

Rousseau, J.-J. (1960). *Les Rêveries Du Promeneur Solitaire*. Paris: Garnier.

Winnicott, D. W (1971). *Playing and Reality*. London: Penguin.

The spiritual dimension in psychotherapeutic practice

Nathan Field

There are two key terms in this paper: psychotherapy and spirituality. Let me begin by indicating what I broadly mean by them. Psychotherapy I see as a practice whose aim is the healing of troubled minds. Spirituality is that ingredient in human behaviour characterized by understanding and compassion, combined with a sense of the sublime, the good, the beautiful, and the true. Having juxtaposed these two sets of ideas, it must seem virtually self-evident that psychotherapy and spirituality are profoundly interconnected, and possibly even different aspects of the same process.

Yet this was not the view proposed by the founder of psycho-analysis. On the contrary, Freud (1911b) promoted the idea that the human psyche was biologically driven by the twin desires for personal survival and sexual gratification and was fundamentally narcissistic; that is, incapable of concern for others, and devoted to the "pleasure principle". As a doctor and scientist he followed Darwin in regarding humankind as primarily members of the animal species: in this context the appreciation of beauty, truth, and goodness was by no means self-evident. Although he later refined this view it remained the basis of the way he saw human nature.

In practice, it is widely acknowledged that Freud was personally devoted to the pursuit of truth, appreciated beauty, and valued goodness. He had his human failings, but was also capable of generosity, and is known to have been deeply troubled by the vast human suffering caused by war. How, then, does he account for these altruistic qualities in himself and in others? According to Freudian theory, they come about through the need to shift, as far as it as possible, from the pleasure principle to the reality principle. Human beings need one another in order to survive, and if we each pursue our own narcissistic goals life becomes intolerable. In the longer term the human species will destroy itself. Providing we learn to live according to the reality principle and can maintain some control over the pleasure principle, human existence will be bearable and what Freud called "neurotic misery" will be reduced to a minimum. He took it for granted that the rational ego was the ultimate judge of what could be deemed reality.

Melanie Klein elaborated on Freud's "pleasure principle" and renamed it the paranoid–schizoid position, which she regarded as the earliest stage of human functioning. Freud's "reality principle" became, in Klein's terminology, the depressive position, and its achievement she regarded as fulfilling the task of psychoanalysis.

In recent years a phase has been identified as prior to Klein's paranoid–schizoid position. This has been provisionally labelled, by the analyst Ogden, the "autistic contiguous" position. He supports his thesis by drawing on the work of child analysts such as Bick, Meltzer, Tustin, Bion, and Winnicott. Autistic–contiguous experiences, according to Ogden,

> are object related in a very specific and very limited sense of the word. The relationship . . . is certainly not a relationship between subjects, as in the depressive mode; nor is it a relationship between objects, as in the paranoid–schizoid mode. Rather it is a relationship of shape to the feeling of enclosure, of beat to the feeling of rhythm, of hardness to the feeling of edgedness . . . there is practically no sense of inside or outside, self and other. [Ogden, 1992]

Thus, Ogden proposes that there are not two positions, but three. The aim of the first position (Ogden's autistic–contiguous) would seem to be *survival*; that of the second (Freud's pleasure principle) would be *gratification*, and the goal of the third (Freud's reality principle) we could call *happiness*, which requires the capacity, as Freud put it, to defer pleasure. What I now wish to propose is the existence of a fourth level. Just as we may well risk survival in our pursuit of pleasure—making the shift from the first to the second level—and just as we can learn to defer pleasure in order to achieve happiness—which constitutes the move from second to the third— I am suggesting that built into the human psyche is the potential to defer both happiness and gratification, if only briefly, for what we might call *meaning*. This constitutes a developmental advance beyond the third dimension to the fourth. It is a possibility to which an increasing number of depth psychologists now subscribe. Among them I would include the psychoanalyst Donald Meltzer, who declared that "the most evolved aspect of an individual's mind lies beyond the experience of self . . ." (Meltzer, 1973, p. 78), and Bion, who claimed that "at-one-ment with ultimate reality is essential to human growth" (Bion, 1970, p. 26). Contrary to Freud, Bion asserted that we cannot know reality, since it is ineffable: we can only become it.

I must make it clear that neither Meltzer nor Bion are referring to religious beliefs but to what are often called "religious", "aesthetic", or "peak" experiences. These may happen only rarely in life but, on closer questioning, they would appear to happen to a great many people, although they are not much talked about. They may be triggered by the sight of a particular painting, a line of poetry, a phrase of music, an intellectual insight, the night sky, the birth of a child, a life-threatening crisis, indeed in a variety of surprising ways but, most commonly, by falling in love. They may also happen in prayer, meditation, and occasionally in the therapeutic encounter. When they occur the individual is briefly precipitated into an ego-transcendent state that is experienced as joyous, even ecstatic, but may also be overwhelming and terrifying, possibly both at once, but above all carries a revelation of a different, and ultimate, reality. A powerful example of such an experience can be found in a description, out of many such recorded statements, by R. M. Bucke, a respected nineteenth century psychiatrist. He was riding home in a hansom cab after an evening spent in deep conversation with two friends, when:

> All at once, without warning of any kind, he found himself wrapped around, as it were, by a flame-coloured cloud. For an

instant he thought of fire—some sudden conflagration in the great city. The next [instant] he knew that the light was within himself.

Directly after there came upon him a sense of exultation, of immense joyousness, accompanied or immediately followed by an intellectual illumination quite impossible to describe. Into his brain streamed one momentary lightning-flash of the Brahmanic Splendour which ever since lightened his life. [Bucke, 1901]

However, joy may not always be the prevailing emotion. In practice the majority of people are profoundly disturbed by such experiences. The loss of their familiar sense of self is felt to be devastating: so in most cases they prefer just to forget what happened, and carry on with their lives as before. It was in this context that T. S. Eliot remarked that "man cannot stand too much reality". There are more fragile personalities who actually become so terrified that they may try to abort the experience, which is like trying to hold back a tidal wave; or they become manically inflated, believing themselves to have been divinely chosen. Either way the experience may leave long-term damage. So it is not surprising that for many years Western psychiatry treated all these non-ordinary experiences as a form of mental illness. But there are also many, like Bucke, who can neither forget nor dismiss what they once glimpsed and come to regard these experiences as defining moments of their existence.

Ego-transcendent experience has often been compared to waking up from a dream, the dream we all habitually live in, that which Bion called "the trance of everyday life". I want to propose, as Bucke did, that this awakening is a natural stage in human development. Just as it is part of the normal growth process to shift beyond the first dimension to the second, and from the second to the third, so it is possible to make a brief shift from the third into the fourth. Each shift—for example, from the pleasure principle to the reality principle, as may progressively happen in psychotherapy—is met with marked resistance. Moreover, because each shift does not nullify its predecessor but can only partially encompass it, no awakening is ever secure: in times of stress we find ourselves under the greatest pressure to return to an earlier level. Bion signals this back-and-forward oscillation in his personal shorthand when he writes "ps← ———→d", meaning that we are always prone to regress from the "depressive" to the "paranoid–schizoid" level, and back again.

In short, I am proposing that we need to look at the human psyche from a broader perspective than hitherto, in that we extend Freud's original two-phase developmental model to a four-phase model, which incorporates what I call the fourth, or "spiritual", dimension.

Historical perspective

We might also apply a much larger perspective to the history of psychotherapy itself. If we simply call it by its original name of *healing*, we realize that psychotherapy did not begin with Freud a century ago, but dates back to the dawn of human society. On the wall of a prehistoric cave at Lascaux, which was occupied over fifteen thousand years ago, is clearly depicted the figure of the healer, or shaman, with his staff, his bird mask and bird claws, etc., to indicate that he believed himself capable of flight to the realm of the spirits, both good and evil. There now exists an extensive literature on the remarkable role of the shaman in human society, a role that survives to this day in pre-technological communities in every part of the world. It is even more intriguing to trace the parallels between shamanism and contemporary psychotherapy.

The shaman's role combined both the healing and the priestly functions. From the very beginning healing combined the mundane and the sacred. (Eliade, 1964) This is evident in the ancient healing procedures universally employed around the Mediteranean basin, especially in Greece and Egypt. They took place in temples or sacred sites, often quite awesome places. The setting aside of certain spaces for supra-mundane purposes has gone on throughout history, such as the Holy of Holies in the ancient Jewish temple in Jerusalem. Something of this same spirit lives on in the therapist's consulting room: it is sealed off from the outside world not just to ensure confidentiality of private matters, but because something special is enacted within it.

Although in our era psychotherapy seeks legitimacy as a para-medical activity, it is interesting to note that originally physical medicine was regarded as a para-spiritual activity; that is, physical healers were usually assistants to the priestly healers. Over many thousands of years spiritual forces have always been enlisted in the treatment of mental and emotional disorders, most commonly by a combination of healing and exorcism. With the rise of medical technology in the eighteenth century spiritual healing fell increasingly into disrepute. It revived with Mesmer's discovery of hypnosis, whereby he cured all manner of hysterical disorders. Hypnosis flourished throughout Europe for over a century, in spite of the fact that the medical establishment found Mesmer's theories quite repugnant. Towards the end of the nineteenth century it gained renewed scientific respectability, especially in France, through Charcot and Bernheim. Breuer used it in his treatment of Anna O, the case that led Freud to invent psychoanalysis. Psychoanalysis, in its turn, has been subject to attack from the mainstream medical and scientific disciplines. Hypnosis has managed to survive and is still practised as a therapy. There is little doubt that psychoanalysis too will survive and, in my view, is destined to play a significant role not only in the treatment of psychological disorder, but in the evolution of the human spirit.

Therapeutic practice and spiritual development

The connection between the earliest healing practices and modern psychotherapy are well worth further exploration. Research into shamanism reveals that many shamans discover, usually in dreams or visions, that only by becoming healers themselves will they be able to cure their own prolonged and mysterious illnesses. Something similar applies in psychotherapy. It is a commonly observed fact that a great many practising psychotherapists have come into the profession by originally seeking help for their personal problems. These are the so-called "wounded healers", and it is through the direct knowledge of their own inner wounds that they are able to help others.

Shamanic training was always conducted by a senior shaman, whose modern equivalent would be the training therapist. The shaman's methods varied with every tribe and every society but, like all initiation processes, they involved some degree of suffering. Demanding initiation rituals still occur in many areas of contemporary life, turning raw recruits into soldiers, for example, or medical students into doctors. It is has been observed that there is an early phase in medical training where the student is convinced he or she suffers from virtually every illness in the text book. Something similar happened in my own experience when I first worked in a mental hospital: the emotional disorders of the patients seemed hardly different from my own. For several weeks I wondered how I had managed to hide my own mental illness all these years? This may sound no more than a lapse into irrationality, but in fact it was a necessary initiation process. It closely echoes the experiences of the trainee shaman in his or her dramatic encounters with both helpful and malign spirits; or as we would say now: in our encounters with the Unconscious.

The training of a shaman, as described in their mythology, involves a symbolic process of dying, being dismembered, and then re-assembled into a new, and more spiritual, form. The ordeals of modern psychotherapy training are a diluted version of a similar procedure, in that they involve an unusual degree of stress, deep feelings of inner disintegration, and gradual re-integration into a resilient practitioner. This occurs in the training analysis and taking on our first training patients. As part of that experience the trainee therapist takes in each patient's illness and must somehow learn to detoxify it. Nowadays, this is described in terms of projective and introjective identifications. In most analytic discussions of these primitive mechanisms the focus is on the one who projects—either the infant into the mother or the patient into the analyst—but here I want to draw attention to the impact on the recipient: the therapist. The containment and processing of noxious introjects I would regard as an inner refining process. By doing so, we become increasingly immune to psychic infection. It is how we learn to identify with the patient's illness but not succumb to it. This renders the therapist an appropriate "new object", available for the patient to interiorize where the original childhood experience went wrong. The passing back of the now detoxified introject may be facilitated by interpretation, but this may not always be necessary, providing the inner connection is in place. Without this connection, with its basis in empathy, interpretation cannot be truly mutative.

Clearly personal development cannot be achieved without some pain. In primitive societies the ordeals of initiation called for the utmost capacity for endurance. But the practice of therapy, although observing Freud's "rule of abstinence", cannot comprise only pain. Counterpoint to the pain there must be some joy. In discussions of the nature of the therapeutic relationship the commonest analogy is of the one between a mother and her baby. When the average healthy mother and her infant can enjoy being together, both flourish. Why shouldn't the same apply to patient and therapist? I think it is in the patient's interest, as well as the therapist's, that we are able to enjoy certain sessions where the partnership feels right, the work feels right and, in the longer term, we can rejoice in seeing a patient improve.

The training, of course, is only the beginning. Winnicott once remarked that it takes ten years after qualification to become a psychotherapist. I think this is an optimistic prediction: in practice we work with what we are, and what we have learned, but the more we learn the more obvious it becomes how much more there is to learn. It means we have to endure working in a state of relative uncertainty.

To arrive at certainty—which in analysis would constitute the ability to offer consistently correct and timely interpretations—would be an immense relief. It is what the analytic training aims to instil in the trainee, what the patient looks for in the psychotherapist, and what we all look for, as therapists, in ourselves. But, in fact, we can only rest in that certainty for the briefest time, otherwise it becomes a *dead certainty* and our interpretations become stale clichés. I am reminded of the anecdote told by Grotstein who, after some years of deep confusion as Bion's supervisee ventured to say: "I think I might just be beginning to understand what you mean . . .". To which Bion replied: "I was afraid of that."

The best that both spirituality and therapy can offer is not certainty but to "have life more abundantly", which involves both pleasure and pain, clarity and confusion. In religious terms it comprises the difference between the religious seeker and the fundamentalist. Fundamentalism is another name for the paranoid–schizoid position. It seeks for the inner peace that certainty seems to promise but cannot deliver, since fundamentalism is saturated with fear and rage.

The therapist who appears to be certain of his understanding, who never blunders but is always in control of the process, actually fails to meet the patient's most basic need, which is to have some-one who really knows their confusion from the inside but can live with it. Nor is this all: since there is a limit to what we can genuinely identify within each patient, we must also have the discernment, as Patrick Casement said earlier in this series, to recognize where they are distinctly other and to respect that "other-ness". The daily practice, as a therapist, of this very difficult balan-cing act could justifiably be regarded as a spiritual discipline.

All the major religions place great emphasis on the individual evolving to a higher level. In this respect Buddhism has, I suggest, the most in common with psychotherapy in that it is the most psychologically minded. The practice of Buddhism requires the student to sit for long periods in a form of meditation known as "mindfulness" practice. This involves deep self-scrutiny and brings meditation close to objective self-awareness. But mindfulness, in Buddhism, involves more than sitting in meditation; it calls for the capacity to live from moment to moment in a mindful way, so that each act in our daily life—eating, breathing, talking, etc.—is done with a spontaneous awareness *of being there.* Judaism has an elab-orate technique to sustain mindfulness by making it a religious obligation to utter blessings in connection with a whole variety of everyday acts. Devout Muslims, whatever they are doing, break off to kneel in prayer five times a day. The difficulty is to sustain the spontaneity and not let the blessings and prayers degenerate into mere mechanical reflexes.

The capacity to be in the "here and now" is widely regarded as the essence of the spiritual attitude. Therapeutic practice actually obliges us to exercise this vigilant self-awareness throughout each hour of the working day. It is this practice that, in my view, consti-tutes the main rationale for focusing on the transference, and, espe-cially, on the counter-transference. The more we are alert to the thoughts, feelings, fantasies, and bodily sensations aroused in ourselves, the more access we have to the patient's inner world, the more they know they are held in mind, the more present we are to them and, at the same time, we are present to ourselves. By these means the therapy becomes a two-way process. The therapeutic relationship is no longer that of a healthy, insightful analyst help-ing a sick, unthinking patient to sort their life out, but a shared venture into the unknown territory of the present moment. By focusing primarily on the interactive process happening in the room, while at the same time trying to correlate it with the patient's material, both therapist and patient are given the opportunity to be most fully alive, alert, and authentic.

Bion, as we know, advocated this state of mind in the most radical way by recommending that we abandon both memory and desire and stay as far as possible in the present moment, in order to focus on the mysterious "O" of the patient. "O", in clinical practice, refers to the fact of the other's ineffable presence, which we can meet only with our own. Essentially it is a meeting of minds, not just brains. As Steven Mendoza pointed out earlier, Bion's notion of "O" belongs in the same mysterious domain as the Buddhist notion of the Void. The Void is a something that, by definition, is no-thing, yet is the foundation of all things. Expressed thus we come up against a paradox. A paradox has been described as "a statement or behaviour that is seemingly inconsistent, absurd or self-contradictory, yet in fact true". In therapy we are frequently faced with paradoxical situations that the mind cannot really grasp any more than we can grasp water. What we can do is let it grasp us. That is to say: surrender to it.

Winnicott described a patient who, for years, remained hopelessly stuck. Finally Winnicott admitted, "I too have no hope that I can help you." The patient replied, "When you said you felt hopeless it was the first time I felt any hope. Let's just carry on." Winnicott's admission was an act of surrender to some unknown process that both he and his patient were engaged in, and was therefore essentially a spiritual action that transformed a long impasse.

In recent years, thanks to analysts, therapists and counsellors working in the spirit of Winnicott and Bion, it would appear that psychotherapy is entering a new phase. Increasingly analytic papers are appearing where the subjectivity of the psychotherapist is taken seriously into account. Patrick Casement long ago touched a nerve in his idea of the therapist learning from the patient. Christopher Bollas goes still further when he writes:

> I am receptive to varying degrees of ".madness" in myself occasioned by life in the patient's environment. . . . In moments such as these who is the patient? In my view much of the work of analysis will have to take place within the analyst, since it is the analyst

who, through his "situational illness", is the patient in greatest need. Indeed, in order to facilitate the analysand's cure, the analyst will often have occasion to treat his own situational illness first. [Bollas, 1987, p. 204]

Current psychoanalytic practice in the USA is increasingly influenced by similar notions of "intersubjectivity" or "relational analysis". Harold Searles, an analyst of an earlier generation, put forward the thesis that his schizophrenic patients had become deeply ill in a failed attempt to heal a psychologically damaged parent (Searles, 1975). He also observed that they improved to the degree that he, Searles, could allow *them* to heal *him*. Conducted in the right spirit, the practice of healing heals the healer. The same theme of mutual influence and mutual benefit is manifest in Jung's remark that "when two chemical substances combine both are altered" (Jung, 1954). One of Jung's great discoveries was his recognition that psychotherapy has more in common with alchemy than with medicine. Alchemy was not simply an elusive dream about turning base metals into gold. Alchemy was essentially a spiritual process whose aim was to turn base emotions into spirit. Psychotherapy offers the same opportunity.

References

Bion,W. R. (1970). *Attention and Interpretation*. London: Tavistock.

Bollas, C. (1987). *The Shadow of the Object*. London: Free Association Books.

Bucke, R. M. (1901). *Cosmic Consciousness*. Innes & Sons [reprinted New York: Dutton, 1969].

Eliade, M. (1964). *Shamanism*. Princeton: Princeton University Press

Freud, S. (1911b). Two principles of mental functioning. *S.E., 12.* London: Hogarth.

Jung, C. G. (1954). *The Psychology of the Transference, C.W., 16.* London: Routledge.

Meltzer, D. (1973). *Sexual States of Mind*. Strath Tay, Perthshire: Clunie Press.

Ogden, T. H. (1992). *The Primitive Edge of Experience*. London: Karnac.

Searles, H. (1975). *Counter-transference and Related Subjects*. Guilford: International Universities Press.

RESPONSE BY JENNIFER SILVERSTONE

I want to thank Nathan Field for asking me to respond to his paper, "The spiritual dimension in psychotherapeutic practice". Doing so has enabled me to think more deeply around the many interesting points that he raises; my aim is not to express a closed or definitive point of view, but rather to open up a discussion. To do this I shall write about the thoughts I have had that were stimulated by his paper, and comment on some linked aspects of his work. I hope by showing how my thinking diverges from his to open up a dialogue with the reader, and a space for further thoughts.

I should make clear that I do not link the practice of psychoanalytic psychotherapy with spirituality. Spirituality I take to mean something that is linked to religious belief in the broadest sense. I make no claim for spirituality in my work nor in the language I shall use to describe it. To best describe the practice of psychotherapy as I aim to practise it I turn to Thomas Ogden:

> the sort of unconscious engagement with the analysand to which I am referring results in the creation of a third subject, the "intersubjective analytic third" . . . the experience of analyst and analysand

[and of] the analytic third represents an experiential base, a pool of unconscious experience to which analyst and analysand both contribute and from which they individually draw in the process of generating their own experience of the analytic relationship. [Ogden, 2001, p. 19]

This thinking enables me to think about retrieving the past, working in the transference and seeking for a truth as something that is subjective and created within the relationship between patient and therapist. The consulting room offers a place free from intrusion, boundaried and constant. It is within this analytic setting that a space for reverie, for thought, and for creativity can take place. The therapeutic goal, as I think of it, is to use that space to bring two minds together and to create from them something different, as paradoxical as Winnicott's transitional object, which is both given and found, old and new, belonging to one and then another, and eventually is discarded by both without rancour. If I have an aim it is to reach that position, or moment. In Ogden's description of creating something new and searching for the truth, he expresses the dilemma thus.

What is true is a discovery as opposed to a creation, and yet, in making that discovery, we alter what we find and, in that sense, create something new . . . In so doing the analyst creates the potential for a new experience of what is true which is derived from the patient's inarticulate unconscious experience. [Ogden, 2003, p. 97]

It seems to me that it is in the making of the "something new" that the analytic process comes to life; furthermore, it is within this new experience that creativity lives.

Nathan Field's book *Breakdown and Breakthrough* (1996) is a clear exposition of his current thinking, and the chapter that to my mind links deeply with his paper, "The spiritual dimension in psychotherapeutic practice" is the one entitled "The fourth dimension". Here he describes, I think, the roots of his thinking about the self, and the self in relation to an other. The fourth dimensional state is not only explored within the psychotherapeutic relationship, it is, he says, a state of being that can be experienced alone or in the presence of another. It can be stimulated by an aesthetic or cultural experience, or simply can be a recognition within the self that something unnameable but separate and distinct from ordinary life has taken place. In the consulting room the fourth dimension presents another way of thinking about the two-person relationship, the coming together of self and other.

From this position, this thinking around self states, he links the idea that if there is mutuality of feeling within this dyad, which he describes as a "simultaneous union and separation of self and other", and he believes there is, or certainly can be, the potential for this state of being in the therapeutic encounter, then the feelings that this state engenders can be both deep and profound, and should be respected primarily as feeling states. He believes that they are different to a sense of "primary fusion in which both the sense of self or the other is diminished or lost". This I take to be a comment on the two-person nature of the interaction, a point we can perhaps come back to in discussion. These states, feeling states, are in his view "characterised by stillness, silence, and intense mutuality. When the four dimensional state occurs in the one-to-one therapeutic setting it carries the conviction that healing has taken place". It seems to me, therefore, that these states of mind, or feeling states are not then disturbed, as it were, for analytic use but left like transitional objects as unclaimed areas of creativity. Once we value this position, and name the process as one of healing, it is not a great leap but a rather small step to get from the fourth dimension into spirituality and other linked states of being and feeling.

Although these may not occur frequently, I think that feelings of an intense linking between self and other, deeper than a meeting of minds or a sense of oneness or closeness, are common to all of us in our experience both in and out of the consulting room. The idea of four dimensionality is, Field explains, different from ideas around the notion of synchronicity, although the two concepts are linked in some ways. For it seems to me that most of these ideas constellate around ideas of fusion, merging, and symbiotic relationships. However, Field defines these feeling states, and indeed makes a passionate case for defining this coming together of the internal and the external, to which he adds thoughts about the soul or the spirit, as a profound shift away from a theory of mind, or a meeting of thinking minds. He defines the fourth dimension thus:

What I argue for is the recognition that four dimensionality exists, that we are encompassed by it as the fish is encompassed by the sea, and that the change of perspective brought about by our awakening to it not only alters our view of life, but enables us to enlist its healing power. [Field, 1996, p. 73]

The idea that others know our mind, understand our feelings, and feel alongside us similar thoughts, are constructs most commonly described as identification and projective identification. I think that both Field and I agree that it is in the most primitive and intense relationships, or moments in the consulting room, that these feelings are aroused and often heightened. These projections are made more complex by the transference and counter-transference, and although they may well be difficult and slow to unravel, projections and projective identifications can be, and indeed are, available for interpretation. I think, too, that we would agree that our severely damaged or borderline patients are the ones most likely to pick up and share and, indeed, challenge the unspoken and unconscious part of the self within the therapist. The baby who lives desperately un-nurtured by a mother with an absence of mind, a mother who cannot hold the idea of the whole-object baby in her mind, or the mother who lacks the capacity to process feelings, deal with the projections, or, indeed, to provide a mind available to the infant, encourages these babies to desperately seek other ways of knowing what is happening in the mind of the mother. Deprived, almost, of one of their senses as they grow into adulthood they may manage their two-person relationships by becoming highly skilled at reading the most subtle changes of tone, nuances and feelings in the therapist. Some of these patients become the most attuned adults, able to sense in a way almost verging on the uncanny, what is going on in the mind of the other. The emotional weather forecast, to be found in the mother/therapist is always taken, and often minute by minute. (For a fuller discussion see Silverstone, 2003). When so much is felt to be at stake, to be abandoned in the void of not being known is too much of a risk, might these patients feel these intense experiences of being known as spiritual?

To return to the description of the fourth dimension, while I admire this description I would like to say something perhaps a little controversial. My sense that this power, or what is described as healing power, may be, and here is the difficulty, a quality that resides in the therapist who contains this dimension as a system of belief. It seems to me that it may be part of, but different from, the capacity to be empathic, part of, but different from, the capacity of the patient to use the therapist as a whole object. To become a good object, or at least to become a useful one in the internal world, there has to be object use, survival, and the capacity to be used by the other ruthlessly. All of these seem to me to be states of mind or qualities that we strive for, states of mind in the therapist that are enabling for the capacity for thinking, reverie, and reflection; states of mind that enable the therapist to reach into his or her unconscious for an un-thought response, but none of these states necessarily would I be able to perceive as having of themselves the capacity to heal. It is, of course, possible, and probable, that these are areas of definition. What I would call in my ordinary practice a moment of deep mutuality, Field may define as a feeling belonging to the fourth dimension. The knowledge that I may have made an interpretation of the mutative kind, responded to in the room with both minds engaged, I may describe as a shared sense of deep satisfaction in the process; might not Field describe this, too, as a fourth dimension?

In his paper Field describes centrally two themes, the double journey of the master and the pupil, student, or trainee, and the parallel path of the therapist and the patient, the priest, and the supplicant. Both these paths, he makes clear, are about the possibility of bearing the unbearable, staying with uncertainty, but above all coming out at the other end unscarred but not unscathed. In so far as the profession of psychotherapy follows this path, and has two central components: a master, or a guide and a follower, a novice to accompany the "other" on a journey, it does link with other journeys that may be both spiritual and disciplined in nature. Here I am grateful for Field's overview of guides and healers and knowledge of shamanism. However, I am cautious about the potential to rarefy the setting, for it is not by definition a hallowed space but rather an uncontaminated space where transferences can flourish and where constancy and familiarity may take on a deeper meaning.

It is, I am sure, true that all of us in the helping professions have to heal ourselves and in part we all start our journey with this internal knowledge, however well we defend against it. My problems with this extended metaphor thesis are twofold. First, healing, to my mind, is a long way from spirituality and spirituality linked with healing seems to me to be problematic. Linking these ideas may encourage a kind of mawkish attachment to the idea that it is only through suffering that some sort of higher order of feeling is attainable.

The second problem posed is that if we privilege suffering and link it with spirituality we are dangerously close to by-passing ideas of rationality and thought. Thought, the development of language, the naming of fears and experiences, enables us to bring the unbearable and unspoken to life; once fears are named they are on the way to becoming graspable. This is not a modern notion, naming has always had significance in the consulting room. It seems to me that words are powerful containers and produce a mutuality of understanding that is as strong or often even stronger than an unnameable feeling. In Winnicottian language we can begin to unravel our relationships to our objects, objects that make up our inner world, when we begin to understand how we place ourselves in relation to them. When we can move from our understanding of how our internal world functions we can begin to explore how that shifts and colours what we loosely call external reality. In order to achieve this task we may create extremely strong feelings in both ourselves and the other. We may engage with sensations and feeling states that are echoes of our very earliest moments; all this is the stuff of psychoanalytic psychotherapy and here I am closer to the often quoted statement, "How can I tell you what I think till I see what I say", than I am to Field's statement of "ego-transcendent experience".

When we understand our position in relation to the object we begin to understand what part we have played in the narrative structure we give to our lives. Analytic structure enables us to begin to understand how we have placed ourselves in our lives and, of course, we are helped in the understanding of the phenomenon by the transference and counter-transference. On all this I think Nathan Field and I would roughly agree.

The other point I want to make is that notions of spirituality can, when overvalued, enable us metaphorically to throw up our hands in horror at the human condition and the spiritual metaphor enables us to remove ourselves from being agents of it, or playing our part within it. The danger of privileging suffering is that it by-passes agency and encourages a defence of not knowing and living in uncertainty. Although not knowing and uncertainty are the stuff of analysis, psychoanalytic psychotherapy, if it has a goal, and to my mind it has, it is to put the unbearable and the unthinkable into language and thence to some form of thought that ultimately can enable understanding and allow for the unknowable to become knowledge and understanding.

There is absolutely no hint in this paper of leaving religious commitment, practice, or feeling unanalysed; and here I absolutely agree with Field's description of the difference between religion and religious fundamentalism, which can be and often is practised as a defence. Sometimes a defence against the negative and some-times what he refers to as techniques to sustain mindfulness (the orthodox Jew saying his blessings, the psychotherapist greeting his patient in silence) are not necessarily what they seem, but can also be carefully structured frames of mind put in place to ward off terror and steady a troubled mind that is desperately attempting to free itself from all manner of bad or distressing thoughts. The constant call to prayer or to acknowledgement of the non-taken-for-granted nature of daily life is a skill that only a few attain and for a great many, certainly those coming into the consulting room, it is often an attempt to keep ordinary life and negative and hateful thoughts at bay.

There are many patients for whom the language, and indeed the concept, of the spiritual and religious are not available. What do we make of these patients? Do they lack the capacity for the fourth dimension or is it simply that this language, this configura-tion of thinking, has no meaning for them? So, too, with religion, or politics, or any set of firmly held ideas, and for some the out-side world has a completely different set of meanings; all these ways of being are challenged, by definition, by the process of analy-sis. Firmly held views across the spectrum of a patient's life will be examined in the process of the journey, their views or feelings may well be re-internalized and valued perhaps more highly, or with greater clarity of feeling, or they may be mourned and lost when they have been re-worked in the process of analysis and found wanting.

I want to end with a question, which I hope will facilitate our discussion, and a comment on my own position. I am now going back to the paper and to the fragment of Winnicott that has been quoted. Here Winnicott has described a patient who for years remained hopelessly stuck; finally Winnicott said: "I too have no hope that I can help you", to which the patient replied: "When you said you felt hopeless it was the first time I felt any hope. Let's just carry on."

Field says, "Winnicott's admission was an act of surrender to some unknown process that both he and his patient were engaged in, and was therefore essentially a spiritual action, which transformed a long impasse." I would be thinking more along the lines that this admission from the therapist freed the patient. That it enabled him possibly in several ways to recognize that he was unconsciously attributing to the therapist a sense that he would always know best, have the map if you like, and this admission freed the patient from this particular set of feelings. It may be that the unbearable, the dread thought, "there is no hope" was put into bearable language. It might then become an intervention over time that could be referred to as a moment of mutuality, a paradox that not knowing about not knowing was ultimately useful and transformative. Now for my question: I have no doubt that Field feels this intervention to be spiritual, and this is perhaps where my difficulty lies; I am not sure what those feelings consist of, and I would like to know. My hunch is that what we have here are two different and possibly equally effective ways of looking at the same piece of material.

As for my response to the question: is psychotherapy a spiritual discipline? I would have to say that for me it is not. Does spirituality have a place within it? I would say not more than any other form of thinking, religion, aesthetic, any set of beliefs felt to be of value to the patient and experienced by her as part of the truth and the authenticity of the self. We cannot and should not as psychotherapists take up a stance where we value one set of ideas, one way of thinking above another. I see the therapeutic encounter as an opportunity to free someone into becoming himself or herself in an authentic way and to bear together whatever the pain of living necessitates.

References

Field, N. (1996). *Breakdown and Breakthrough*. London: Routledge.

Ogden, T. H. (2001). *Conversations at the Frontier of Dreaming*. London: Karnac.

Ogden, T. H. (2003). What is true and whose idea was it? *International Journal of Psychoanalysis, 84*(3): 593–606.

Silverstone, J. (2003). An absence of mind. In: B. Bishop, A. Foster, J. Klein and V. O'Connell (eds.), *Ideas in Practice*. London: Karnac.

The use of theological concepts in psychoanalytic understanding

Ronald Britton

The great American scholar, M. H. Abrams (1973) wrote that the romantic writers of two hundred years ago, such as Goethe, Wordsworth, Holderlin, or Shelley, undertook to save traditional concepts by reformulating them within a two-term system of subject and object, man and nature. A hundred years later Freud suggested that one could venture to resolve religious myths, and transform metaphysics into metapsychology, by the psychoanalytic understanding of the unconscious. I accept Freud's premise that the internal world described in psychoanalysis was represented in theology in terms of the relationship of the individual to his Creator. I believe that we confront in our work similar problems of the inner and outer world but in earlier centuries we addressed such problems in theological terms. Therefore, I find it useful, when trying to understand problematic transference and countertransference situations, to draw on theological concepts such as Justification and Grace, and rival belief systems such as Idolatry and Fundamentalism.

The relation of the subjective self to internal objects, such as the superego, provides us with interesting analytic insights into the nature of religious beliefs. From the beginning of the twentieth century psychoanalysis was the principal method of exploring areas of mental life that previously were the concern of philosophers, poets, and, most of all, theologians. Before the eighteenth century Enlightenment, the issues of psychic life that today concern psychoanalysts were formulated in theological terms. Then, for a time during the Enlightenment, reason alone reigned and the irrational and the supernatural were omitted from the agenda. In the period that immediately followed the Enlightenment, the philosophers and writers of the romantic movement tried to reintroduce ideas previously expressed in terms of the relation of man to God in their account of man's relationship to nature and to himself. They sought explanations in personal history, rather than in heaven. A century later, Freud continued and transformed this process. He added to their method of seeking the truth in the depths of their own minds the possibility of seeking it by exploring the depths of other people's minds. As contemporary analysts we too have been privileged to continue and add to that process. We encounter the same issues in analytic practice but we think of them in our own terms. However, in my work with patients, I have also found it useful to reverse this process, seeking to understand some prevailing transference relationships by exploring religious doctrine.

I will give an example: it concerns the problems of two particular patients who had an urgent and recurrent need to justify themselves by their achievements. They were both highly successful in very different fields of activity. They had accumulated prestige and reputation, but both felt that they must repeatedly produce something new that would impress everyone or they were condemned. This affected them both profoundly in their everyday lives and work, but in the analysis it was, for a long period, manifested in the counter-transference. It was I who repeatedly felt a need to justify myself. When, after some time, I was able to recognize my problem and not just suffer from it, I put to myself a question: why did I feel in every session an urgent need to try to produce something brilliant in order to survive as the patient's analyst? Previous achievement counted for nothing. It felt as if I started from zero every day. I was able to use this counter-transference experience, eventually, to understand that for both of these patients this was the state of affairs that existed for them in their lives, but in the sessions they functioned as receivers of doubtful goods from a dubious source.

I contrasted this with my experience with other patients and it helped me to realise that feeling justified was a state of mind I usually possessed and I only seemed to lack it in these two analyses. Having found this word 'justify', I recollected the enormous importance that had been attached to the doctrine of Justification in the Christian religion and what controversy it had caused. This led me to explore the doctrine and the long dispute that had arisen about it.

Justification and the State of Grace

Justification means, in religious terms, being freed from the penalty of sin and made righteous by God. It was a key term for both Catholic and Protestant theologians and was one of the most contentious concepts of the Reformation. The doctrine of Justification occupied as central a position in sixteenth century theological debate as did the relationship of the ego to the superego in the mid-twentieth century psychoanalytic "Controversial discussions" in London. The Protestant position, expounded by Martin Luther, was that "justification by faith alone" sufficed for salvation. A most extreme form of this belief was expressed subsequently by Antinomian Protestant sects that those with true faith need not abide by *any* laws, as they were already saved and sanctified. I am sure that many analysts have met patients, and perhaps even colleagues, who appear to follow that creed in relation to psychoanalysis. You need only believe to be saved. Calvin's version of justification by faith alone was more logical but more terrible: in so far as faith was a gift from God and clearly not possessed by everyone, some individuals were predestined to salvation and others to damnation. Those fortunate enough to possess the gift of true faith were the elect. (Are there echoes of that doctrine too in the colleges of psychoanalysis?) Other Christians, like many in that broadest of churches, the Anglican community, took the position that Justification could simply be achieved by good works, provided these were modestly dedicated and attributed to God.

None of the psychological counterparts of these theological positions was open as a route to Justification for my two patients. They did not have the gift of sustained faith in anything, certainly not in psychoanalysis, as a means of their salvation. Others might possibly profit from it, but not them. Nor could they believe that any quantity of good work would save them from the sense of unworthiness. In fact, one was a gifted and highly praised artist, the other a very successful financier. But no amount of good work gave the artist a sense of being a good artist and nor did any amount of success in business give my other patient a sense of being a good financier.

In religious terms this state is most easily understood in the Catholic doctrine of Justification. Essentially, that doctrine propounds that though good works are in themselves meritorious in God's eyes, the individual performing them does not gain merit unless he or she is in a State of Grace. Good behaviour alone does not redeem, and redemption is what they were both seeking in their lives and in their analyses. Phrases from the liturgy capture the desirable state of mind regarded as the state of grace: ". . . that they may truly please Thee, pour upon them the continual dew of Thy blessing". The psychological counterpart to the continual dew of God's blessing was singularly lacking for both of my patients. Hence the desperate urge to repeat meritorious acts. What they had in common was a belief that if they did not repeat their successes daily they were damned; one expected to be exposed as a fundamentally hopeless person, the other, in some indefinable sense, a bad person. Neither of my patients believed themselves to be in a state of grace.

But what is this state of grace in psychoanalytic terms? Freud has, I suggest, already told us in his memorable observation: "to the ego therefore, living means the same as being loved, being loved by the superego" (Freud, 1923a). If the ego feels hated by the superego it abandons its hold on life. He writes: "The superego fulfils the same function that was called for by the father and later by providence or destiny" (ibid). Although Freud relates this to the father, in the same passage, interestingly, he traces its genesis to the anxiety due to separation from the protective mother. If we consult theology, it tells us that grace is a supernatural gift of God by which we are made children of God and pleasing in his sight. Both my patients believed profoundly that they were not loved, understood, or wanted as infants. In the transference this eventually became manifest: they believed that they were not wanted by me

for themselves but only as a source of gratification for my professional narcissism. They were not victims of the Devil; that is, they
were not paranoid but melancholic, the subjects of a cruel God. In
their internal oedipal configuration the third position was occupied
by a god of adverse judgements. It is a reminder perhaps that in the
Oedipus myth itself the original sin of Oedipus, in the eyes of his
father Laius, was simply to have been born.

God the Father and God the Mother

Freud, in his paper on Leonardo da Vinci, said "Psychoanalysis has
taught us that the personal God is psychologically nothing other
than a magnified father" (Freud, 1910c). He regarded monotheism
as a great achievement of the Jews because it took them beyond
polytheism and nearer to what he thought was religion's true
origin: the father nucleus. He said, "Now that God was a single person, man's relationship to him could recover the intimacy and
intensity of the child's relation to the father". The infantile supremacy of the father complex has been questioned, and with it the
reasons for God the Father being placed in solitary state on the
heavenly throne. Barag (1947) suggested that Jewish monotheism
was impelled by a defensive repudiation of an otherwise dangerous
mother fixation. In Kleinian terms this would be the removal from
the mother of the attributed qualities of omnipotence, omnipres-
ence, and omniscience, and a transfer of them first to the father, and
then to God the Father. Thus, these supernatural qualities are taken
from their infantile source in the mother, whose body is the proto-
type of the natural world, Mother Earth, and attributed to the
Father in Heaven.

There is a hint of this transfer in a paper Freud wrote called "On
a 17th century demonological neurosis" (Freud, 1923d). It concerns
an artist who suffered a psychotic breakdown in which he saw the
Devil, and it appears that while God might be unambiguously a
father, the Devil's gender is more doubtful. Freud took the view in
this paper that God and the Devil were originally one figure, but
later became divided into absolute goodness and absolute evil
personified. The artist Christoph Haitzmann painted his hallucina-
tory meetings with the Devil, with whom he had concluded a rather

curious pact that, after a period of nine years, he would become "the son of his body". Freud postulated that the Devil was a substitute for the painter's lost father, an explanation in line with Freud's own father complex.

However Freud drew attention to something in the paintings that struck him as strange: the Devil had breasts. In one picture, in addition to breasts, he had a large penis ending in a snake. Freud offers alternative explanations for this: one is that the breasts are a projection on to the father of Haitzmann's own femininity. Then he offers another, that the child's strong fixation on his mother had been displaced on to his father Indeed, Haitzmann himself had declared that only the Holy Mother of God could release him from his pact with the Devil on the day of her nativity. The way I read this is that only the physical appearance of Mary in her own form as the Holy Mother, distinct and separate from God the Father, could save him, because the Devil was a fantasy of what Klein called a "combined object".

Klein wrote that the infant's capacity to enjoy its relation to both parents depends on his feeling that they are separate individuals. The fantasy of a combined object is frequently terrifying. For some infants, establishing a distinction between an unequivocally good and unequivocally bad experience is difficult. Therefore, instituting the normal primal split between a good and a bad object is a compromise. If that is so, then I think that all other distinctions between the parental objects are compromised and prone to fusion and confusion. If this has been the case, then regression in later life can lead to the re-emergence of primitive fantasies of combined objects or, alternatively, to disintegration. This in turn leads to arbitrarily imposed defensive splitting in order to keep apart these archaic objects and the different values they represent.

Fundamentalism and idolatry

I think a dream of a patient of mine might make this a bit clearer: in his dream my patient was holding in one hand a candelabra and in the other a vase. His associations revealed that the candelabra was from his father's piano and the vase was one his mother had always locked away because it was an heirloom from her own mother. In his dream he slowly brought his hands together and as they touched both objects disintegrated into tiny fragments. Such was the nature of his internal object relationships that the bringing together of his maternal relationship with his relationship with his father did not produce psychic integration but disintegration. The fear of such a catastrophe can lead to a ruthlessly self-imposed division of the mind to keep things apart, often along some pre-determined or natural line of cleavage, such as the boundaries formed by different modes of self-object experiences. Such a line of cleavage, I suggest, is that between a parental object experienced as the source of solace and comfort and a parental object perceived as the source of knowledge. Goodness is then felt to reside either in material objects or in pure spirit, the two often seen as conflicting powers. I think this holds true in religion, philosophy, and political ideology.

There is a common tendency in all religions for conflict to arise between a sacramental theology with emphasis on material objects, ritual practices and sacred places and an anti-material, idealistic, textural, spiritual Puritanism. In Catholic doctrine the attempt is made to bind word and thing within the sacrament: "The word sacrament means something sacred or holy, the outward signs of the sacraments not only signify grace, they actually impart the grace they signify" (Hart, 1916). When, in a baptism, we see the priest pouring the water and hear the words that he pronounces, we know that the soul of the child is at that very moment *really* cleansed from original sin. Such an attribution of sacred signifi-cance to a physical substance is regarded as idolatrous by those Pro-testants who regard Biblical text alone as holy, and spiritual activity as exemplified only in words: prayer, preaching, and reading. I see this as reflecting a psychic conflict between, on the one hand, the earliest attachment to a maternal object (later represented by sacred material objects and related activities) and, on the other, a father object represented as the source of words, power, and the law. I am inclined to think that such latent conflict becomes supercharged when confusion threatens and moral certainty is lost.

I am further suggesting that this particular split into different modes of relating, though institutionalized by the psychic manipu-lation of the Oedipus situation into worship of an earthly mother or a spiritual father, actually has its origins in the primary maternal object. In this latter relationship, when there is a failure to establish an unequivocally good experience of the infant–mother interaction and a contrasting bad experience when deprived of it, some arbitrary split is made to enshrine the notion of good and to segregate it from the bad. In a context where there is a passionate desire for the mother's presence and an overwhelming need for her functions as a mother, but an actual experience of a dysfunctional relationship, the concept of a good maternal object might be salvaged by treating her as two figures: one a presence and the other a function; one regarded as goodness and the other as badness.

I have encountered this split both ways around. You could schematize it as a division that does not result in a good breast and a bad breast; you have instead either a good breast with bad milk, or good milk from a bad breast. I have found the clinical permutations of this, in the individual psychopathology of addiction, perversions, and eating disorders in particular, very fascinating. But here I want to use it to explore what I am calling Fundamentalism on the one hand and Idolatry on the other. The term "fundamentalism" is commonplace nowadays, but it derived originally from a series of Protestant tracts published in the USA in 1909. The fundamentals were based on the authority of the infallibility of the Bible, claiming that every word in it is the word of God. That movement had two particular objects of enmity—Roman Catholicism and Modernism. Roman Catholicism was regarded as idolatrous, particularly in regard to the central doctrine of the "real presence" in the sacramental bread and wine, signifying the body and blood of Christ; Modernism was hated for its emphasis on secular justice, individual freedom, and physical well-being.

The term "fundamentalism" is now applied widely to a variety of religions: Christianity, Judaism, and Islam. In all of them it usually denotes literalism and the worship of religious text. It is almost invariably accompanied by condemnation of modernism linked with materialism, and of idolatry. Christendom and Islam, interestingly, have both had civil wars between the puritan members of their religion and those co-religionists whom they accused of idolatry.

I regard fundamentalism simply as "word worship" and idolatry as "thing worship". This institutionalized splitting leads to difficulties of integration in the individual in the depressive position and hence a failure to symbolize. The true symbol, as it was under-stood particularly in the romantic movement, is very similar to the one understood in psychoanalysis: that is, as the meeting place of meaning and matter, spirit and substance. It is the place where something is simultaneously what it is in its substance, and also in what it signifies. The symbol is more than a signifier and more than a metaphor. As Coleridge put it, "It always partakes of the reality of the original which it renders intelligible, and while it enunciates the whole, abides itself as a living part in that unity of which it is the representative" (Coburn, 1967). This sounds very abstract, so let me put it into commonplace experience.

As an analyst my experience of how I am regarded varies with each patient. One of the parameters of this variation is how much of my actual physical and mental self is included by the patient in the transference. Another way of putting this might be to say: how much of my manifest existence is included in the patient's concep-tion of me and how much am I a product of the patient's mind? Here we have materialism and idealism in practice. When all goes well, I feel perceived as recognizably myself, doing more or less what I think I am doing, and yet know that in a way peculiar to this particular patient, at this particular time, I am shaped into a trans-ference figure. There is always a tension in it. I think the symbol is always the point of tension where ideas and things meet. But in a reasonably favourable analytic situation, the co-existence of my patient's ideas about me and my sense of myself are tolerably close. It is not always so in every analysis and with some patients it may not be so for a very long time.

I want to discuss the situation where there is an extreme discrep-ancy between the patient's idea of the analyst and the analyst's idea of himself. It is in such discrepant situations, when the normal process of interaction between fantasy and reality breaks down, that fundamentalism or idolatry appear. They appear, I believe, where internal and external objects are felt to be not only incom-patible, but that one will be the death of the other. On the one hand, the counter-transference fantasy of the analyst is that if he adopts the psychic reality of his patient, his own psychic reality will be annihilated. On the other hand, the patient believes that if the analyst asserts his version of their shared situation, this will crush and eliminate the patient's sense of self. The only way out of such an impasse is by the analyst's recognition of the nature of his own counter-transference anxiety, and his need to struggle to accommodate both his own and, at the same time, the patient's psychic reality. It is very difficult work, but it needs to be done. Otherwise the analyst will try to compel the patient to accept his reality, and since this is the process that created the patient's problems in the first place, it is fruitless!

It was my failure to contain just such a situation that first really acquainted me with the dimensions of this problem. This all followed an interpretation of mine in which I said to my patient that she seemed to wish to have a physically contiguous and continuous relationship with me. I then added that this would not serve her well because it required my eternal presence, and that what she needed was to take in some understanding, so that she had it available inside. Ms A. took my interpretation to be a pronouncement. She believed that I had attacked her mode of relating to me and that I sought to impose on her, in its place, my religion. As she saw it, I was forbidding the one kind of link she really believed in and was demanding instead that she accept my words as gospel. Her reaction was a violent severance of verbal contact with me. This at times extended to her removing herself physically from the consulting room, and other times just silence. This evolved, for the both of us, into a sense of desolation. It left her without any vital link to an outside figure, and any attempt on my part to establish verbal connections was likely to lead to further ruptures.

Her own solution was to form a relationship to me that excluded those elements which she could not tolerate and to enhance those she could. I would call the transference relationship that she established idolatry. I was, as an idol, the source of goodness. My physical presence, including the contents and walls of my room, were the principal elements of this idolatrous relationship. She managed to include in it my words, by treating them as conveying only sound but not meaning. She treated my voice as a source of tactile quality such as soft or hard, splitting her object world into different sensory modalities, and treating these different perceptions as if they came from different people.

She further institutionalized this segregation by attaching these different relationships to the different members of the basic Oedipus situation. Thus, words had become father's thing in a round of ideas without substance or texture. Mother's thing, on the other hand, had substance, shape, texture, and qualities such as colour, softness, warmth, firmness, and pliability that provided comfort and security but not meaning. In the light of this, I would like to discuss further this polarization into fundamentalism and idolatry, or word worship and thing worship. In the former, word worship, the words of the text are treated as powerful, sacred, and inviolable, transcending their function of simply conveying their meaning approximately. In thing worship or idolatry, the thing itself, the material object is treated as possessing psychic or supernatural power.

In his paper "The unconscious", Freud (1915e), in attempting to describe the form of representation in the conscious and unconscious mind, distinguishes between word representation and thing representation. He believed that in a normal state of affairs the two are brought together in the pre-conscious mind and it is this conjunction that gives them potential for consciousness. But when they are separate, word representation is pre-conscious and thing representation, he thought, is unconscious. However, he adds something very interesting. He suggested that in schizophrenia it was different. Repression in this condition, he wrote, had nothing in common with the repression in transference neurosis. He thought that in schizophrenia the ego had taken flight, thus abolishing any potential connection with even the representation of the thing itself. Instead, word representation was given the investment and significance that usually belongs to things. Thus, word abstractions were treated as things. Interestingly, things were treated only as ideas. So in the schizophrenic mental world words are the real thing, language is a form of action, and to name it is to do it. In contrast, thing representations are only the furniture of thought. And Freud added "When we think in abstractions, there is a danger that we may neglect the relation of words to unconscious thing presentations and it must be confessed that the expression and content of our philosophizing then comes to acquire an unwelcome resemblance to the mode of operation of schizophrenics" (*ibid.*). His final comment on this was even more perspicacious. He suggested that the endowment of words with thing status was an attempt to cure: "an endeavour", he wrote, "directed towards regaining the lost object" (*ibid.*). In his paper on the theory of dreams (Freud, 1915b) written immediately after "The unconscious", he suggested that hallucination in schizophrenia may also be an attempt at restitution, this time of the lost ideas about objects. Thus, he proposes that in schizophrenia words may be endowed with supernatural power to restore the lost internal object they signify, and hallucination may be an attempt to reinstate it by representing it externally in the perceptual world. It is not without significance that these two papers were written together with his great paper on "Mourning and melancholia" (Freud, 1915c). In all three of these papers he makes a connection between the loss of the primal object and the process which either gives thing status to words or perceptual status to thoughts. This is so whether the primal object is lost from the individual's external world as a person or whether it is lost as an internal object.

If we use the concept of non-verbal unconscious phantasy for what Freud called thing representation, which I would prefer to do, it becomes easier to discuss it. Unconscious phantasy, as envisaged by Melanie Klein, refers to the mental representation of wishes and needs, somatic and perceptual experiences, anxieties and other affects. Most of all, unconscious phantasy creates what we call internal objects, some of which Freud described as being incorporated into the ego, that is, into the sense of ourselves, and others into the superego, a particular location for internal objects that have the attributes of conscience. Thinking of ourselves beginning as infants, you could say we began as believers in animism. Subsequently we have to distinguish between living and non-living things, which is an accomplishment. The further development that leads us to the notion that there are thinking things other than ourselves, which have independently their own subjective mental life, is actually another considerable achievement. I don't think we manage it all the time. The full acceptance of the fact that other people's minds are just as real as our own is something that we find difficult, and we vary at different times and in different situations in our ability to truly accept it. Some personalities actually find other psychic realities very threatening to their own psychic reality, which they hold either tenuously or very fiercely.

It is this conception of another person with a separate mind that fully achieves what Melanie Klein meant by a "whole object": that is, a whole person with different parts and functions. But we begin our lives not with whole but with part-objects which are simply personifications of simple ideas or qualities; and part equals whole. You might say that at that stage we have angry gods, loving gods, jealous gods, or cruel gods. In a most primitive part-object relationship only the experienced moment exists and only that part of the object immediately perceived has any existence. Here there is only a sense of the object as a total world, and in relation to this primitive object there is only one mode of relating: either I am inside it, or it is inside me. The first form of projection is of the total self into the object, and the most primitive introjection is the incorporation of the entire object into the self. Desire for union is expressed as a fantasy of total self projection or total incorporation. As William Blake put it, " I am in you and you are in me—mutual in love divine", when he was characterizing the mental state he said could be found in Beulah, his imaginary earthly launching pad for the return to paradise. And he added, moreover, that Beulah could also be found in each district as "the beloved infant in his mother's bosom, round and circled" (Keynes, 1959).

The negative of this loving union is total repulsion. I repel the object or the object repels me and when the absoluteness of part-object relating applies, if I repel the object it is annihilated and if the perceived object repels me, my perceiving self is annihilated. The fear, therefore, is of annihilation. This potential state of affairs begins to change when two developments in infantile mentation occur: one when the primary object acquires continuity of existence so that it goes on existing even when not perceived, and the other when the self is perceived as separate from the object. Then, and only then, we can in fantasy put parts of ourselves into others, while continuing to exist outside them. And we can receive from others without being appropriated. At this point function and being can be separated. "I am" becomes separable from "I am eating" or "I am evacuating". Being is no longer identical with doing, having, or knowing. Ontological identity can co-exist with epistemic identity and self-awareness can complement self-existence without threatening to obliterate it.

The negotiation of this step in development depends on what Bion described as containment; a process that he believed depended on the maternal capacity to introject the infant's projections and the infant's capacity to tolerate the mother's containing function. These infantile capacities for containment, he thought, could be interfered with, in some personalities, by envy. Bion's ideas about infantile containment were based mainly on his analysis of adult borderline patients. I have suggested (Britton, 1998, p. 58) that the problems of containment evident in such personalities is a resultant of two factors: one is the maternal response to infantile projected identification and the other an innate factor in the infant.

In *Belief and Imagination* I suggested that this innate factor in the infant was a hyper-sensitivity of what I think of as the psychic immune system, a kind of psychic atopia, a hyper-sensitivity to psychic difference, an allergy to the products of other minds. In analysis this sensitivity applied not only to minute variations in the analyst, but also to approximations in understanding. Where this sensitivity is considerable, what is required in the way of understanding is perfect understanding. Anything less than perfect understanding is perceived as misunderstanding. In analysis such a situation can be relived and repeated when the patient attempts to communicate to the analyst by projective identification and feels that the analyst fails to introject and therefore annihilates the patient's attempt to find meaning, seeking instead to enforce an alien understanding in the form of words. It was just such a situation with Ms A, described earlier in this paper: she regarded words as anathema and cultivated a form of analytic idolatry, the symbols of which gave her a feeling of supernatural union.

This patient could be described as belonging to the group of narcissistic disorders that Rosenfeld described as "thin-skinned". These two clinical states, the "thin-skinned" and the "thick-skinned" are the result of two different relationships of the subjective self to the third object within the internal Oedipus situation. In both states the third object is alien to the subjective sensitive self. In the thin-skinned mode the self seeks to avoid the objectivity of the third object and clings to subjectivity. In the thick-skinned situation the self instead identifies with the third object and adopts its mode of objectivity, renouncing in the process its own subjectivity. I think that the hyper-objective, thick-skinned mode of transference relating, avoiding subjectivity, has a theological counterpart in the predilection to fundamentalism. It involves a wish to find salvation in the realm of the word, a purified supernatural belief liberated from the matrix of personal interaction and free of sensuous symbolic resonance. In contrast, the hyper-subjective transference mode resembles an essentially idolatrous worship of the person whose supernatural presence is believed to protect; it can inhabit any number of material residues and critical substances, transforming them into fetish objects.

Put briefly, in personalities where for innate or environmental reasons mother's psychic functions and her physical presence have not been integrated into one good object, splitting produces a good maternal presence coupled with a bad maternal function; or vice versa. That is then replicated in the transference, where it takes the form of, on the one hand, an analytic idolatry, or on the other, an analytic fundamentalism. In the former the analyst is personally idolized with a craving for his physical presence or its token: in the latter, there is an idealization of the analyst's words and presumed thoughts that is often coupled with a hidden aversion to the analyst's actual presence. I have suggested that this sort of splitting can be found not only in individuals but in societies, where it can be expressed in theology, in philosophy, or in political ideology. Psychoanalytic theory is not exempt from this. Nor are psychoanalytic societies any less prone to idolatry or fundamentalism than other human organizations. Our knowledge, after all, does not protect us from such transference phenomena. It only offers us the opportunity to be aware of it. We can, I am sure describe vividly the resistance we find in our patients to such enlightenment. And if we are honest I think we can all testify to such resistance in ourselves.

References

Abrams, M. H. (1971). *Natural Supernaturalism*. New York: W.W.Norton & Co.

Barag, G. (1947). The question of Jewish monotheism. *Imago, IV*: 8–25.

Britton, R. (1998). *Belief and Imagination*. London: Karnac.

Coburn, K. (Ed.) (1967). *Coleridge: a Collection of Critical Essays*. Englewood Cliffs, NJ: Prentice-Hall.

Freud, S. (1910c). Leonardo da Vinci and a memory of his childhood. *S.E., X1*: 59–138.

Freud, S. (1915b). A metaphysical supplement to the theory of dreams. *S.E., X1V*: 217–222.

Freud, S. (1915c). Mourning and melancholia, *S.E.*, *X1X*: 237–243.

Freud, S. (1915e). The unconscious. *S.E.*, *X1V*: 202–204.

Freud, S. (1923a). The ego and the id. *S.E.*, *X1X*.

Freud, S. (1923d). A 17th century demonological neurosis. *S.E.*, *X1X*: 69ff.

Hart, C. (1916). *The Students Catholic Doctrine*. London: Burns Oates and Washbourne.

Keynes, G. (Ed.) (1959). *Blake: Complete Writings*. Oxford: Oxford University Press.

RESPONSE BY HESTER SOLOMON

"So what she gives God, she gives from earth's two faces,
the pain, the festival; the tense surprise of sound and metre
knitting.
And then is what she gives to us, clear under God's sky—
The priesthood of her caring"

Rowan Williams, Angharad

Spirituality and pathology

With the elegance and depth that we have come to associate with his widely respected contributions over the years, Ron Britton has spoken on a psychoanalytic understanding of idolatry and fundamentalism. He makes the interesting distinction between the "word worship" of fundamentalism and the "thing worship" of idolatry. Juxtaposing Freud's notion that ordinarily word presentation and thing presentation are brought together in the pre-conscious, giving them the potential for consciousness, he contrasts this with the situation found in highly pathological states such as schizophrenia, where word representation takes on the equivalence of thing representation. Here, abstractions are treated as things, and concrete things as abstract. He evokes Melanie Klein's concept of unconscious phantasy, in which internal objects become incorporated either into the ego, which he calls our sense of self, our "core self", or into the superego, which he describes as a particular location for internal objects with which the self is related. The internal objects that inhabit the ego become our sense of "our hearts and souls", giving us a shape in the world and protecting us from it. In describing the primitive state of part-object psychic reality, on the other hand, he notes that personifications of single ideas take on the diverse identities that belong to a panoply of mythological figures, such as angry gods, loving gods, jealous gods, or cruel gods. This is, of course, a way of describing what Jungians would identify as archetypal psychic contents, universal themes that we, by virtue of being human, all experience according to our capacities and inclinations.

Ron Britton is one of a growing number of psychoanalysts who have turned to the concept of the self in order to explore certain types of clinical phenomena that cannot be described in other terms, including the structural terms of id, ego, and superego. Within this exploration are included those primitive mental states variously called narcissistic, borderline, and schizoid phenomena. Regretfully, where this exploration of a notion of the self occurs, the terms of reference are held almost exclusively within recent psychoanalytic writing, despite the long and ongoing Jungian analytic tradition of theoretical and clinical enquiry into the nature and dynamics of the self. This was based on Jung's own experience of such primitive states in his work as Psychiatric Director of the Burgholzli Hospital in Zurich. One example of this would be my own view, clearly Jungian, in which I would not equate the sense of "our hearts and souls" solely to the ego, even if this aspect is nominated as "our core self"; nor would I equate our sense of the panoply of gods, even if these include negative ones, solely to the superego.

Although early in his paper Ron Britton identifies the self as the "core ego", in a later section he states: "In this primitive object world there is only one mode of relating: either I am inside it or it is inside me. The first form of projection is of the total self into the object and the most primitive introjection is the incorporation of the entire object into the self . . . a phantasy of total self-projection or incorporation." In this latter quotation, he seems to refer to the self in the Jungian sense as the totality of the being of the individual and its central dynamic—in Jung's famous dictum, "The self is to the ego as the mover to the moved".

Britton's concept is similar to one that Jung earlier employed to think about the impulse for union as giving rise to terror of the devouring mother. In this case, the defence against this threatening psychic state must be found in its opposite—total repulsion or schizoid withdrawal. Again, we are in the realm of the archetypal defences, where the absoluteness of part-object relating, as Britton indicates, results in the phantasy of an either/or situation whereby if I repel the object it is annihilated, or if the object repels me I am annihilated. The real birth of the self as a separate identity occurs "when the self is perceived as separate from the object. . . . we can in fantasy put parts of ourselves into others, while continuing to exist outside them. And we can receive from others without being appropriated. . . . Being is no longer identical with doing, having, or knowing. Ontological identity can co-exist with epistemic identity and self-awareness can complement self-existence without threatening to obliterate it". Again, as Jung said, "The self is to the ego as the mover to the moved".

Britton's thoughtful analysis of the vicissitudes of containment usefully includes not only the maternal capacity to introject the infant's projections, but also the infant's capacity to tolerate the mother's containing function, a capacity which can be interfered with by envy. Too much innate envy can lead to a kind of "hyper-sensitivity [of the psychic immune system] to psychic difference . . . an allergy to the products of other minds . . . [when] less than perfect understanding is perceived as misunderstanding" (Britton, 1998). If the analyst fails to introject this internal situation, the patient's attempt to find meaning is thereby annihilated. When the patient requires the perfect understanding of the analyst, which would be the equivalent of psychic union or fusion (what Britton calls a "supernatural union"), the patient is manifesting "thin-skinned narcissism", typical of the borderline personality. Following Rosenfeld, Britton distinguishes this from "thick-skinned narcissism", which is predominantly schizoid. He considers that the hyper-objective thick-skinned mode of transference relating has a theological counterpart in a predilection to fundamentalism, a wish to find salvation in the realm of the word, free of sensuous, symbolic resonance. In contrast, the hyper-subjective transference mode resembles an essentially idolatrous worship of the person whose supernatural presence is believed to inhabit any number of material residues and physical symbols.

Fundamentalism and idolatry are based on those psychic defences erected for the protection of the self in circumstances where, as Britton states, "for innate or environmental reasons, mother's psychic functions and her physical presence have not been integrated into one good object". Hatred and fear ensure obedience to the fundamental premise that the self will not survive without adherence to the strictures of the defensive system. Ron Britton has offered us a most convincing account of the internal state of affairs that leads to the establishment of the modes of fundamentalism and idolatry that can keep the psyche in thrall and imprisoned. He has described what Jungians would call archetypal defences of the self, those self-care systems set up to ensure the psyche's survival in the face of dire internal or external circumstances. He has thereby contributed to our understanding of such psychic situations by describing how, in the clinical setting, the analytic work can be thwarted at every turn, when a combined object can be morphed at any moment into its opposite, such as the good mother with bad milk, or the bad mother with good milk.

Ron Britton ends by reminding us that psychoanalytic societies are no less prone to idolatry or fundamentalism than any other human organization. He counsels us to be mindful of the inevitable resistances to our awareness of the ubiquity of such psychic retreats from the possibilities of the more benign forms of relating, internally and externally. This holds as much between our analytic societies as within them, and in particular between our Freudian and Jungian groups.

Spirituality and health

I want to broaden out our attention to include an underlying interest of many of us who have followed this series throughout the year, and to think about the sources of spirituality from a broader point of view, identifiable as a primary psychic function, ubiquitous throughout history and across cultures, thus archetypal in nature. In this view, although it is accepted that some aspects of spiritual experience might be found in repression, hatred, idolatry or fundamentalism, when this occurs we might understand it as a perversion of what we might also wish to convey when we think of spirituality. Ordinarily, I think we associate spirituality with something more *aspirational* (the *telos* of the person as the self unfolds into its future) and *inspirational* (in the Greek sense of breathing in of something Divine, something godlike), which are powered by such universal but not consistently available human emotions as love, devotion, reverence, and the willingness to sacrifice. Of course, these may only appear with struggle and discipline over time, and of course there are enormous impediments that get in the way of their realization, through exactly those systems of psychic defences that Ron Britton has defined as fundamentalism or idolatry.

But what about the other side of the coin, those more benign functions within human capacity that can enable good enough caregivers to provide for environments that facilitate, as opposed to frustrate, and those more benign innate capacities that may provide an internal weighting more on the side of growth and development, notwithstanding inevitable blocks and adverse internal systems? How are we to take account of these, given that they are also with us by nature of our very humanness?

A profound interest in understanding the origins of the universal human impulse to turn to religion and spirituality motivated both Freud and Jung and constituted much of what caused their tragic split. They were in a race to publish their findings, Freud experiencing excruciating difficulty in writing his version (Kresse-Rosen, 1993) and Jung keeping very quiet about his progress. The impact of their split continues to exert seismic effects in our contemporary analytic organizations. We could say that, since Freud, within psychoanalytic circles the topic of the origins of religion and spirituality was subsequently more or less eschewed until recent efforts, notably from Ron Britton, and indeed from others included in this series of seminars. Jung and a number of those who followed him remained constant in the search to deepen our understanding of these issues, which are central to the dynamics and processes of meaning making of the human spirit, and so often a motivator of actions for good and for ill, as the unfolding of recent events has made so apparent.

I wish to emphasize that it is impossible to deny the importance and existence of the dreadful internal state of affairs that give rise to the kind of malign forces such as Ron Britton has described. Moreover, he has delicately refrained from linking his insights into the origins of fundamentalism and idolatry to their externalization and projection in some of the most terrifying global situations that we face today, but the links are clear, I am sure, to us all. In the struggle in the consulting room, each of us must grapple with these malign states hour in and hour out, and it is fundamental to our work that we seek to understand and face these as effectively as we are able. It is our overall understanding of the interplay of the malign and benign forces, the conditions under which their relative immanence will be revealed, that is the stuff of analytic understanding.

In concluding this response to Ron Britton, I would like to ask some essential questions in this area of our interest, namely, how do love, devotion, reverence, and sacrifice become available, at times, internally to an individual and between two people in the consulting room? In other contexts I have considered how an ethical attitude, which is an integral part of the analytic attitude, can be made available to an individual, or a couple, in an analytic relationship (Solomon, 2003)? We do not require that our patients exhibit towards us, as their analyst, the same ethical stance that we adopt towards them or towards the analytic relationship. This essentially ethical (because not contingent on the other's response to us) analytic attitude allows for the eventual emergence of exactly the sort of psychic contents that Ron Britton has been talking about today—narcissistic, borderline, and psychotic states—that are, in essence, ruthless because they are essentially non-relational. In the face of these manifestations the analyst adopts a non-retaliatory stance that requires varying degrees of self-sacrifice as he or she remains open and receptive to the impact of the psychic contents of the patient, while at the same time cleaving to an essentially ethical attitude.

How and why do we do it?

In thinking about the acquisition of spiritual, including ethical and other altruistic behaviour that happens, despite those ruthless self care systems that Ron Britton has explored, I have described (Solomon, 2003) the situation that pertains when a combined parental function, characterized by devotion and thoughtfulness, provides a non-contingent situation in which a dependent but developing self is free to become more and more an authentic self in relation to others. Where such provision fails, self-care systems are put into place, such as idolatry and fundamentalism, that shore up the self as a way of ensuring survival. This is a view that allows for the ongoing viability of the self as it individuates over a lifetime, including those inevitable cyclical episodes of deintegration and sometimes disintegration (Fordham, 1985), which in another context Ron Britton (1998) has described as the recurrent cyclical pattern of the passage from the paranoid–schizoid position to the depressive position and back again, eternally repeated, that allows for gradual development in the face of inevitable regression. He has given us a vivid snapshot of states where the depressive position breaks down, when systems of idolatry and fundamentalism take over in order to defend against disintegration. In complementary fashion I have offered here a speculation about what might happen when, at times, the psyche is strong enough, endowed enough, robust enough, and inspired enough to reach into other realms, of creativity and capacity for considered freedom and uncontingent devotion and sacrifice, that we attribute to higher forms of spirituality.

References

Britton, R. (1998). *Belief and Imagination.* London: Routledge.
Fordham, M. (1985). *Explorations into the Self.* London: Academic Press.
Kresse-Rosen, N. (1993). *Trois Figures de la passion.* Paris: Springer Verlag.
Solomon, H. M. (2003). The origins of the ethical attitude. In: H. M. Solomon & M. Twyman (eds.), *The Ethical Attitude in Analytic Practice.* London: Free Association Books.

A new anatomy of spirituality

Clinical and political demands the psychotherapist cannot ignore

Andrew Samuels

Introduction

The bigger and more important the theme, the more personal the author's connection to it is likely to be. So I will begin by sketching my personal development in connection with the themes of this chapter. At about the age of eighteen, I was a highly political young man, but trying to realize my political dreams through the arts—specifically, theatre. We were a radical theatre company, in those days at the end of the 1960s when you could get money from the Arts Council for radical theatre companies. Then, after becoming a youth worker and a counsellor working with young people, I went into analysis and dropped out of the political world for a decade. So, when Thatcherism came in, I was busy writing Jungian books. Gradually, the political side of my personality and my interest in society came back in and merged with my analytic concerns, leading to the formation of "Psychotherapists and Counsellors for Social Responsibility". Then, when I began to have children, a third strand came in that we could call "spiritual", as often seems to happen with men. Psychotherapy, politics, and spirituality—three sides of a coin! After the impact of having children, and the turning towards organized religion and private religion fatherhood induced in me, I began trying to link up the practice of psychotherapy with my emerging spiritual and existing political concerns.

I will begin this chapter by discussing some general issues and problems of definition. This is necessary when engaging with what I have heard called the "S" word. Next, I will present an immodestly entitled "new anatomy of spirituality". The third section is on responsibility, and how that links to psychological and spiritual concerns. The word "responsibility" is important to my thinking. Finally, inevitably, given my Jungian background, I feel that I must talk on the shadow of spirituality. We Jungians started the psychotherapy world off on what seems like its new line of taking spirituality seriously. But we always knew that, alongside the gold, there's something potentially wrong with a spiritual approach. So, paradoxically, Jungians are prominent these days in addressing what's the matter with the spirit, as well as what's great about it.

The "S" word

When Captain Cook's ship *The Endeavour* anchored in Botany Bay a little over a couple of hundred years ago, the aboriginal people did not recognize it as a ship because it was simply so big and so different from what they had in their mind as "ship". We don't know what they did think, but we know they didn't think it was a ship. It was only when the smaller longboats—rowing boats—were lowered into the water that the aboriginal observers of this scene realized that there were boats involved, and that there were people in the boats. Spirituality, if we are trying to define it, is something like that. We don't really know that we are in that area until something happens to alert us to it. In Bani Shorter's memorable phrase, everything is "susceptible to the sacred" (1995). This is a very good one-liner to indicate what happens before you can term something spiritual. Something has to happen that involves you "clocking it", to use the modern argot. For everything can be susceptible to the sacred. It is significant that the lectures upon which this book is based were not given in a church, or synagogue, ashram, mosque, or temple. We were in a lecture hall in a psychotherapy training organization. And that setting influenced what we said and what we experienced.

In the new anatomy of spirituality, I seek to advance a vision of spirituality that is regular, ubiquitous, and permeates every aspect of existence. It is not intended to be a lofty, exhortative, sermonizing approach. Quite the opposite. My take on spirituality discerns its worm-like nature, not its eagle-like nature. Spirituality as an underneath as well as an over-the-top thing. And because approaches to spirituality so easily go over the top, it is often better to stay underneath.

So we can scarcely attempt a factual definition of spirituality. We can only give an aspirational one, and therefore whatever we say will be very vague. But there is huge value in vagueness—so much so that there is a philosophical sub-discipline called "vague studies" and even a *Journal of Vague Studies*. I actually think this is a very important lesson for psychotherapists, especially British psychoanalytic psychotherapists and psychoanalysts. We get terribly hooked on spurious precision when it comes to words, spending much time and energy on the differences between guilt and depression, envy, and jealousy, and so on. We speak and write as if we really know, and as if we can really make hard and fast distinctions. It is a kind of love affair, of a very perverse kind, with precision, and I believe it is deeply problematic, clinically and intellectually. There is something important about staying in the vague for as long as it takes. There are obviously dangers of vagueness but I think that spirituality may not be as dangerous a topic when it is regarded in a vague way as some others because, after all, spirituality has always been something that deconstructs our lives. Long before postmodernism was invented, the spirit was deconstructing daily reality in culture. Hence it is not a problem for me that I am vague about what I mean, or what anyone means by spirituality.

I will leave definition there, caught up in vagueness, thinking of Captain Cook, inviting readers to imagine themselves as those aboriginal people. And the longboats are slowly being lowered into the water, and recognition is gradually dawning.

A new anatomy of spirituality

There are four aspects to spirituality and the spiritual dimensions of experience that I shall consider: social spirituality, craft spirituality, democratic spirituality, and profane spirituality. In *social spirituality*, people come together to take responsible action in the social sphere, doing this in concert with other people. When this happens, something spiritual comes into being. Being actively engaged in a social, political, cultural, or ethical issue, together with others, initiates the spiritual. This is a very different perspective from one that would see social spirituality as being something done in the social domain by spiritual people. On the contrary, there is a kind of spiritual rain that can descend on people who get involved in politics and social issues with others—hence "social" spirituality—in a certain kind of way, which I've designated as responsible. The difference should be clear: this is by no means an elitist perspective. Social spirituality embraces people who get involved with other people in political and social action—for example, the whole post-Seattle protest against global capitalism that our young people are getting into. What they're doing when they get involved in the anti-capitalist movements and the environmental and ecological movements is to participate in a general resacralization of culture. To play on the word "politicized", they are becoming "spiritualized". When one gets involved in politics, sometimes—not always—one gets spiritualized. And so the anti-capitalist movement is creating its own spirituality and, in turn, being informed by the spirituality that it creates in a feedback loop. Political action leads to spirituality of some kind, and spirituality informs political action. Of course, eventually it all falls to pieces. Either the police wreck it or people grow up. But there is a basic resacralizing tendency worth recognizing (Samuels, 1993).

In analysis and psychotherapy there are aspects of this social spirituality that we need to consider. Surely we no longer indulge in the typical therapeutic manoeuvre, when faced with a client who wants to go on a demonstration, of interpreting the anti-parental nature of that move, or understand political participation as defensive, resistant, avoidance, splitting, and so on. If there are people in our profession who still make knee-jerk interpretations of that kind, then what I would say to them is that they are caught up in yesterday's good practice. But such a clinical perspective is today's bad practice and ignores the individuating thrust in the client's political and social commitments and actions. What this means, for example, is that, when you take an initial history or when you meet a client for the first time or when you're interviewing a potential trainee, you don't ask: "Well, why were you so involved in politics when you were eighteen?" Do ask: "Why were you not? And why have you apparently got no social commitments at all? Do you read the newspaper? Do you watch Newsnight?" I realize this reverses the way that most therapists have been trained to proceed.

I have written extensively about what happens when political themes enter the psychotherapy dialogue (most recently, 2003). Succinctly, within certain limits, the engagement of therapist and client in relation to something political can be mutually transformative. This is truly another example of social spirituality. In the therapeutic setting, as the therapist and client engage on 9/11, or the Hutton Report, or Princess Diana, or the decline of the Labour Party, they can find—if they are open to it—a deeply transformative experience that may have a spiritual feel to it, in spite of the fact that the raw material was social, political, controversial, and difficult to deal with for all the technical reasons we know about. For we don't want to dominate our clients. The difficulties involved are highlighted by the fact that there are very few texts that help therapists to work in this area.

Before moving on to discuss craft spirituality, I want to touch on the pressing contemporary political problematic of martyrdom in general and suicide bombing in particular. This is a testing topic when thinking about social spirituality. Clearly, for those involved in it, the act of suicide bombing leads to the most profound spiritual transformation on the part of the bomber, no matter how wrong the act is from the point of view of their victims, or of people in the West who simply cannot comprehend how such a thing can come about. Actually, we need to be very careful here, because suicide bombing is not an integral part of any culture that I know of. It is a situational response to a complex sociopolitical situation. But our Western culture cannot comprehend how that came about in other cultures. Martyrdom nudges us up against some of the shadow aspects of spirituality, encouraging us to remember, in any rush to embrace the spiritual and bring it into our work and lives, that martyrdom and acts like suicide bombing are the most extreme, over-literalized form of social spirituality imaginable. We need to bear in mind, before rushing blindly into political and social action, that there is a place it can go that is really quite horrific.

Now for *craft spirituality*. My thesis here is a bit startling: holiness is artificial. It is not something that we merely discover or find in our lives, or notice in God or nature, or in the psyche. We make holiness. We make it traditionally by building tabernacles, and churches, and by performing rituals—lighting candles, holding each other and so on.

To illustrate this point I want to reflect on the biblical figure of Bezaleel. Many people have never heard of Bezaleel, though there is a Bezaleel Institute in Tel Aviv. Bezaleel was the man who actually *made* the Tabernacle and the Ark of the Covenant. He made them to God's precise instructions. When we consider these instructions, we may come to two quite different conclusions. One is that God is the most unbelievable obsessional neurotic! The other is that it really matters to God what is made by us in pursuit of holiness: what materials we use, what dimensions we go for, what bevels, joints, and other technical devices we employ.

> And Bezaleel made the ark of shittim wood, two cubits and a half was the length of it and a cubit and a half the breadth of it, and a cubit and a half the height of it. And he overlaid it with pure gold within and without, and made a crown of gold to it round about. As he cast for it four rings of gold to be set by the four corners of it, even two rings upon the one side of it and two rings upon the other side of it. And he made staves of shittim wood, and overlaid them with gold. And he put the staves into the rings by the side of the ark to bear the ark. [Exodus 37, 1–5]

Such work—maybe, potentially, all work—is a spiritual discipline. In our societies in the West, much work is meaningless and alienating. Nevertheless, even within the meaninglessness and alienation of contemporary work situations, people often develop and deploy a Bezaleel consciousness. They fashion portable tabernacles and sanctuaries for themselves, usually by ritual, often obsessional seeming: how you line up your pens, what colour pen you prefer to write in, how you close down your computer, which people you greet, and in what way. None of this does away with the appalling barbarism of capitalist work organization, but all of it shows people trying to enter the domain of craft spirituality. Craft spirituality also spills over into aesthetics. Craft spirituality informs the artistic and creative impulse as well.

A great deal of this is very relevant to modern psychotherapy but, again, there do not seem to be very many books or papers about it. In fact, there is a lack of psychotherapy literature in connection with work and employment issues. This is somewhat surprising in that clients regularly talk about problems at work. I have hardly ever worked with a client who has unambivalently admired their boss! Rather, those clients that have admired their boss without ambivalence have usually been hopelessly in love with him or her, which isn't much use either.

There are special issues for women in connection with work: the glass ceiling, the appalling continuing differentiation of wage rates, the enormous difficulty in getting the present Chancellor of the Exchequer and the Inland Revenue to engage with the issue of tax relief for child care which, although it should not be a "woman's issue", impacts more on the social and work lives of women than of men. A psychotherapist who does not engage with a woman client in those areas is not only guilty of a social omission, they are guilty of a spiritual omission as well. Because work—craft spirituality—cannot be split off from spirituality as such.

There certainly are craft spirituality issues for men as well. Most private practice psychotherapists don't see many manual labourers. But we do see the children of manual labourers. That's the harsh social fact about it, in private practice anyway. Have you noticed how difficult it can be for the more successful son to come to terms with what that means in relation to the apparently less successful father, who may be by now part of a long-term unemployed, rust-belt declining industry in the North?

For both men and women, there is a very overt spiritual theme that has to do with work, which has been given the unprepossessing tag of work–life balance. (I must declare an interest here as a Trustee of the Work–Life Balance Trust.) There is a sense in which work–life balance may be *the* issue of our time. This includes more than having an annual go-home-on-time day! It's much more than just addressing the chronic workaholism of the population—something that most psychotherapists know about as well, because it's a problem a lot of us have. Getting your work and your personal life into some kind of balance is a *spiritual* matter and not only a social matter. Without decent work–life balance, can anyone really flower as a spiritual being, as a person with a soul? Yet work–life balance is not really discussed by psychotherapists. It is discussed by occupational psychologists, of course, and it's increasingly interesting to economists and accountants. For companies that have effective policies on work–life balance do very well financially. Profit is by no means the right reason to go in for work–life balance but there is a bottom-line aspect that makes it more likely that this movement could have some social and political success. My main point here, when discussing craft spirituality, is to suggest that work–life balance be understood more and more as a spiritual and psychological matter.

I hope it is becoming clearer what I am aiming at in this chapter. This is a contemporary take on spirituality, so that it can become "useful", if you like, in apparently non-spiritual places: in the therapy room, in society, and in people's personal lives.

Third in the anatomy is *democratic spirituality*. This involves the bringing back on to all kinds of agendas—personal, political, and clinical—of the idea of *absolute equality*. In all the discussions about equality of outcome and equality of opportunity, something has got lost. And that is this notion of absolute equality, which used to be called traditionally "equality in the eyes of the Lord". We are all equal in the eyes of the Lord. This is a powerful idea, because it underpins any protest about economic inequality and the situation in the wider world in which women and children die because of economic policies undertaken by their governments at the behest of the World Bank or the International Monetary Fund. Democratic spirituality puts the notion of absolute equality, in all its glorious impracticability, back on to the agenda. In particular, democratic spirituality is an attempt from the spiritual end of the spectrum to engage with poverty, economic injustice, and economic inequality. From the standpoint of psychotherapy, there's a great deal that should be said but usually is not. With some notable exceptions in humanistic and integrative psychotherapy, and among people working in transcultural psychotherapy, psychotherapists in Britain, especially psychoanalytical therapists and psychoanalysts, are not adept at working with power issues in therapy. We still tend to prefer to put the client's challenge to us down to their trouble with a powerful mother, phallic mother, great mother, terrible mother, omnipotent breast, or a castrating, law-giving father who says "No". But there are power issues in the therapy relationship itself that, if overlooked, prevent a certain kind of spiritual communication between therapist and client from taking place. The idea of absolute equality, impractical as I admit, is an ethical penetration of the psychotherapy relationship that leads to an enhancement of the spiritual experience that it can generate.

A couple of final points in relation to democratic spirituality. The first reflects the influence of psychoanalytic thinking on spiritual thinking. In relational psychoanalysis, which is the promising new variant of psychoanalysis that is coming into this country from the United States associated with the name of Stephen Mitchell, the tools exist to describe a particular kind of democratic psychological relationship with God. If you like, this is a relational spirituality, in which one might surrender to the divine, but without masochistically submitting to it. Surrender, but not submission. This relational spirituality, coupled with what I have been saying about democracy and spirituality, is very suggestive and important for therapists. We discern a "non-submissive, non-masochistic sense of veneration", in ourselves and our clients, to use the evocative language of Rosemary Gordon's very important paper on this topic (Gordon, 1989, pp. 237–254). Being able to worship without having to masochistically submit to authority is a part of contemporary spirituality.

The last in the four was *profane spirituality*. Profane spirituality is about drugs, sex, and rock-and-roll. In 1961 Jung replied to a query from Bill W., the founder of Alcoholics Anonymous, with a critically important letter in which he advanced the idea that alcoholism was a spiritual quest that had gone off the rails. This insight can be applied to so many other addictions, up to and including shopping and workaholism. For the avoidance of doubt, perhaps I should make it plain that I am not saying that shopping is a spiritual activity. What I am saying is that there is a strand of energy in the act of shopping that connects to all the searching and questing that spirituality is commonly associated with.

Regarding rock-and-roll, I mean to propose in a shorthand way that we can locate the spiritual drive in popular culture, not only music but also movies and sport. There is a spiritual component here, not really different from that which the intellectual authorities of the world locate in Rembrandt or Wagner or art from the Orient. There is something in what the kids do, and what we did when we were kids (and, I hope, we still do) that should not be put down by reference to "the canon", as they call it in the big debate about what you should study in literary studies. The canon is Shakespeare and Dickens. The anti-canon is Danielle Steele. Although you can get MAs in America in Danielle Steele, I am not going down that track. What I want to say is that, if one talks about profane spirituality, popular culture plays a central part.

Profane spirituality involves sex and sexuality. There is usually a spiritual level in deeply intimate relationships. Psychotherapists need to say more about what it does to the human spirit to enter the domains of alterity, to really confront the other in her or his ethical otherness. And how this leads to self-discovery, and how God-discovery weaves its way through all of it. But I am not only referring to relationships, I am thinking about sex itself—orgasmic, orgiastic, rapturous, to the point of mysticism. That is important because so many mystics write about their mystical experiences in the most frank sexual imagery. There is something about the sex act—just sex as a drive, not sex as part of a relationship—that people who engage with the spiritual would often like to overlook. Here one must (still, regrettably) assert that homosexual sex acts bring a spiritual element with them just as often, or just as seldom, as heterosexual sex acts. Profane spirituality is decidedly not something that goes on only within the sanctity of heterosexual marriage.

The implications of profane spirituality for psychotherapy are enormous. Psychotherapists are becoming fascinated with the body, with neuro-biology and neuro-anatomy. Some even refer to neuro-psychoanalysis. It is seriously argued that the structure of the brain can be affected by what happens to an individual as a client in therapy. It is even more seriously argued that something happens to the structure of the brain in those early months and years of life. Our psychology has become absolutely obsessed with the body. And yet body therapy hardly gets a look-in. There is something very problematic here. We need to go back to those old debates about touch and movement in therapy. The body is the grounding for spirit. But just because it is such a grounding should not mean that we then put it on one side as something noticed but not taken up. We know about the body and counter-transference, and how the somatic states in the therapist are really useful in understanding the psychological states in the client. We know about psychosomatic medicine. In fact, we often say indecent things in our clinical papers that offend the sufferers of various illnesses by proclaiming them to be little more than depression in disguise.

So we are correctly body obsessed. Yet how many of us have regularly—not just occasionally—noticed the breathing of our clients? How many therapists reading this have observed the breathing of the client in therapy? How many of you have actually said anything about it? Or explored your own? Some time ago, I decided to systematically observe the breathing of my clients and my own and I noted that, if I do this, the therapy dialogue alters whether I do anything with what I've noticed or not. Sometimes, I do speak about it. It seems to me absurd to have all these developments that take the whole field in a bodily direction, except in relation to practice! William Blake said, "Man has no body distinct from his soul." So can there really be any psychotherapy worth its salt that isn't in some sense a body psychotherapy?

I want to end this section on sex and sexuality with a few transcultural points in connection with the body—because one of the interesting things about the body is that there is no such thing as a body. There is only my body or your body in this particular society in this particular year. We should listen to colleagues who do transcultural or intercultural work. Here in the West, we talk about people somaticizing their depression: they are depressed and they produce a whole variety of physical symptoms that are really their depression in disguise. At a famous conference of psychoanalysts in India in the late 1950s, one of the Indian participants got up and said: actually the trouble is not that people somaticize depression, but that you in the West psychologize it. For us (he said), depression is always already a bodily state. The Western approach to depression, before and after *Mourning and Melancholia*, is the odd thing in the situation here. Once, in Brazil, I met with indigenous people, and one person said to me as he had said to others: "We always had spirit, it was you Westerners, the Portuguese, who brought the body." And everybody knows about how mind, spirit, and body have got separated in Western culture. There is much to learn from non-Western sources about this kind of thing (see Samuels, 2002).

Responsibility

The words "responsible" or "responsibility" come from the Latin root *spondere*—to pledge. The dictionary refers to being held to account, being morally responsible for one's actions and, interestingly, answerable to a criminal charge. If you are responsible for something, then there's a perpetual sense that you are answering a charge, that something is "wrong". These etymological roots mean that responsibility can only ever be a dialectical business. One cannot really be responsible if there isn't another with whom or towards whom one is responsible.

People give themselves much too hard a task when it comes to responsibility. They lose sight of the very important psychological, spiritual, and political notion of good-enoughness. My preference is not to use Winnicott's notion of good-enoughness developmentally. To me, there is a whole possibility of refreshing the spiritual and political vocabulary bound up with the notion of good-enoughness; for example, the good-enough leader, who admits that she or he will fail and sees as their primary task the management of failure, who will try—to play with Winnicott's words—to fail the country in the country's own way. Or the good-enough citizen, who recognizes that alone one can do so little but with other people one can achieve much more. I suggest "responsible-enough" should be "good-enough" for most of us. This idea brings with it a change that makes notions of responsibility more feasible, more achievable. Good-enoughness in relation to one's sense of responsibility involves self-forgiveness and atonement. And these things are what lie behind the Hebrew word *Tikkun*, meaning the restoration and repair of the world. But we cannot rehabilitate the world if we are so hard on ourselves that we see ourselves only as permanently fractured. We can only move to restore and repair the world on the basis of self-forgiveness and atonement. As Samuel Becket put it: "no matter, try again, fail again, fail better". We have to try to fail better.

The shadow of spirituality

There is something not only all right about spirituality. It is not just that there's a good "mature spirituality", to use the unfortunate title of a recent book, for that would imply there was an immature spirituality. I think there's something not right about spirituality *per se* locked in there with all that beauty and holiness. Look at the evidence. Spiritualty is deployed by mass movements of particularly nasty kinds. It is there in every fascistic movement as well as in less dramatic mass movements. One can see why, because the spirit is part of "the mass". But, because it's part of the mass, spirit is easily assimilable to mindless, destructive, collective political and social actions. I wouldn't say this is due to humanity's defects, that the spirit is all right, but we poor inadequates misuse it. It is more fundamental, this shadow of spirit and there is something in spirit that is permanently not grounded and hence can cause damage. When spirit is not grounded (and, on this thesis, it *never* is wholly grounded), it gets you into states where you will do things that are horrible before you can catch yourself and stop yourself from doing it.

"Spiritual people" often display indifference to suffering. I believe this is also true in the psychotherapy world, where you have people who are very compassionate to their clients, but extremely uncompassionate to any individuals beyond that, including colleagues. Because a person's mind is on higher or deeper things, you are not going to be terribly concerned with other people. Then we need to recall the way in which spiritual leaders seem so often to go on power trips. This is the problem of the guru, about which there's a considerable literature now. The root literature for many studies of the psychological kind of guru-ism are those researches of violent gangs that were done in the 1950s. Everything that was discovered about violent gangs in New York City in the 1950s is directly relevant to the study of guru-led cults that went completely off the rails in the past fifty years.

Another element in the shadow of spirituality is élitism. The spiritual individual feels better than other people. Why have vows of obedience and humility and poverty to be made if not to control their opposites? All taboos imply the impulses that need to be tabooed. Spiritual people who take vows of humility are acknowledging in the act of taking the vow of humility that, if allowed to get away with it, they will be anything but humble. Such is the élitism that is the ineluctable shadow of spirituality.

To illustrate spiritual élitism, I will mention something from my own experience. After my father died, papers arrived including a buff file that had on the outside the legend "*Andrew Samuels—writings*". In this file were letters and so forth dating from long before I became a writer. In this file was a letter that I wrote when I was on what we now call my gap year in Swaziland, Southern Africa. I went out there, lied about my age and got a job in the colonial civil service as an Assistant District Commissioner. I went off into the bush to do what we called a "human resources survey" in connection with rural community development. There, I wrote a letter to my parents slagging off the Western family in general, and ours in particular, saying how I had discovered, living in the *ad hoc* extended family that one finds when you go into an African village (and they are very pleased to see you and take you into their homes) that here, in Africa, are families where people do get on! I wrote about the impact this was having on me. And I used the word spirituality in that connection. I remember being terribly, terribly pleased with this letter. It is long, elaborate, and adeptly (if destructively) put together. But when I read it again in my father's file, I thought: You little shit! What nasty, élitist side-swipes. What grandiosity. What an abuse of the spiritual dimension of life.

Continuing to explore the personal aspect of the shadow of spirituality, I would like to share a dream which, as I understand it, is about the body and about my struggle to keep spirit and body in some kind of related linkage. It is my initial dream from my analysis, dating from September 1971. I dreamt this on the exact date the Germans invaded Poland in 1939—and my family comes from Poland.

> Dream: I am on the deck of a Soviet-style (but not Russian) ice-breaker. We are in a northern sea, the ice-covered Baltic, or the Skaggerak, or somewhere up there. The sea is flat, and the ice-breaker is breaking the ice. I am on the bridge of it. I look out and I see shooting up through the ice great gushing spouts of volcanic-type flame, but there's no volcano, mostly golden coloured flame. I am awestruck by the concatenation, the combination of the natural landscape, of the flat ice, and (from the literal point of view) the unreal thrusting upwards of the golden spouts of flame. Something makes me look down at my body. I am naked. I look at my genitals and there I see a rather crude leather pouch covering them and compressing them. I reach down and, very gently remove it, and put it on one side.

I return to this dream over and over again, not only in connection with these writings on spirituality, but in connection with many aspects of my life. I share it now because the note on which I want to end this talk is about the central significance and challenge of facilitating the body side of things and the spirit side of things into a dialogical relationship.

References

Gordon, R. (1989). Masochism: the shadow side of the archetypal need to venerate and worship. In: A. Samuels (Ed.), *Psychopathology: Contemporary Jungian Perspectives*. London: Karnac.

Jung, C. G. (1973). Letter to Bill W. In: G Adler (Ed.) in collaboration with Aniela Jaffé, *C. G. Jung Letters Volume 2*. London: Routledge.

Samuels, A. (1993). *The Political Psyche*. London: Routledge.

Samuels, A. (2002). The hidden politics of healing: foreign dimensions of domestic practice. *American Imago, 59*(4).

Shorter, B. (1995). *Susceptible to the Sacred*. London: Routledge.

The role of projective identification in the formation of *Weltanschauung*

Donald Meltzer

I will try to stick to this implication that I am going to talk about projective identification, but I can't promise that it will be like that, because what I'm really occupied with these days is the contrast between invention and discovery, which I think is terribly important for psychoanalysis. I'll try to explain why. It is a great consolation to me to read that other people have difficulties with this matter. I was given an article from the *Review of Literature* called "On not being able to play the piano". I thought to myself, I know all about that. But it was very consoling because it was written by somebody who had really obviously broken his heart trying to learn to play the piano well. I thought to myself, if I could play it at all I'd be thrilled. It is the same thing with invention and discovery. In grazing through some mathematical books—which I cannot read but can only graze through—on the subject of negative and imaginary numbers, I realized that I was constantly hearing an equivocation as to whether this was about invention or about discovery. Well, I hope it's not so vague in relation to psychoanalysis. I think, perhaps a bit heartlessly, I would classify Freud as being on the border—being a great discoverer but also a great inventor. The invention has to do really with nomenclature—the names that you give to things, and the fact that names become so concrete and so factual that one does really believe that they mean something. Projective identification is one of these things that you believe in. This raises questions about religion and spirituality—the whole question of belief. Was it Wittgenstein or was it Bertrand Russell who said that the correct linguistic method for expressing something is not "I can see that cat" but "I am cat-perceptive"? That seems to me to be quite correct. But to say "I am cat-perceptive" seems too trivial really for such an effort at correctness.

Last night, thinking over what I was going to say this morning, I was reviewing some of the miracles that I have encountered in my life. I thought, "I'm not cat-perceptive, I'm miracle-perceptive"; and that's something spiritual. The fact that I'm approaching eighty makes it clear really that something has been happening to me that has to do with miracles. For one thing people are much nicer to me than they used to be. I no longer have a car; instead people get up and offer me a seat on the bus. It is very striking to me that people are very nice to me as I get feebler and feebler. It must be also that I am nicer myself, although I have several patients who tell me that I am terrible—that I am evil, that I am brutal, that I am aggressive. And they're so right that you can't argue about it. Something has happened to my vocabulary that is so pointed, so sharp, that it can leave people bleeding a little. But it is not nice to say to somebody: "You're so egocentric and vain that there's no possibility of . . ." and so on. It may be true, but it is not polite. And it's not civilized.

So this benefit I've discovered—that people are nicer to me now I'm rather old and feeble—also makes me nicer to them, and ready to listen to people who tell me how nasty and aggressive I am—all of which Mrs Klein knew very well, so it's not a surprise to me. It is a surprise that people don't kill you when you're like that. I have one patient who always seems to be going for my jugular, but somehow she just barks and it doesn't make me bleed; and I look forward to seeing her next time when she comes and barks at me. I can see that she makes some progress. Every once in a while a little bit of softness slips out of her. But to anyone hearing the session from the hall outside my door it must really sound like murder.

To get back to this serious business of invention and discovery . . . which takes us directly to the differentiation between talent and genius. Talent is one of these miracles that are thrillingly more and more apparent as I grow older. I was looking at a book of drawings by a five-and-a-half-year-old autistic girl who drew horses better than Pietro della Francesca, better than Uccello, and how she could draw these horses was a miracle. They were full of muscle, full of vitality; yet she looked so lacking in vitality herself in the photograph. When I was younger I thought that talent was simply a matter of good teaching and hard work, and that if you persevered you would discover your talents. It took a long time to realize that it didn't work like that. I had good teachers and I worked hard, but nothing happened. What did happen seemed so trivial that it was hardly worth mentioning: I discovered that I was a good reader of dreams, which seems utterly trivial—except that they are marvellous and mysterious and alert you to the fact that the human mind is something about which we actually know nothing. All this business about the double helix is supposed to tell you exactly about the different mental capacities that are imprinted in every cell of your body. There is something too utterly simplistic about it. One need only think about the Bach family or the Bernoulli family to realize that it is not only about heredity but about culture, and God knows what culture means. I certainly don't know. But you are immersed in your family culture from at least before you were born. The discovery that there are children who never get born is a really important discovery—who do not make the transition from dependence on the placenta to dependence on the breast, with the result that they have no access to the communications that Bion has spelled out in terms of maternal reverie and so on. I certainly think I have seen children who failed to get born. Some of them are the kind of children who are called hyperactive and manifest an absolute incapacity for symbol-formation or thought. But how it comes about I can't say.

About how it *doesn't* come about I could say something. I think I have discovered something about the creativity of small children, and how it is connected with their earliest experiences of defecation; with what an achievement and triumph it is for a small child to produce a firm stool, and how it is required that this achievement be recognized. And most mothers do automatically recognize this achievement. But they don't recognize, as it were, the mechanics of it. What does a child have to do or avoid doing in order to produce a well-formed stool, which also turns out to be a good-smelling stool? One discovers things like the role of procrastination in children being incontinent of faeces; where the urge to defecate is not so mandatory that you can't postpone it and postpone it until it is too late, and before you know it you have filled your pants. Not only filled your pants, but it stinks. What the child apparently has to discover is not only not to procrastinate, but its opposite—to be patient, and to wait until his organ is ready to produce a well-formed stool.

Now this brings us really, like Cupid's arrow, back to the problem of identification and, I suppose, to love. To produce a well-formed, sweet-smelling stool is a gift of love. And to be unable to do it is a terrible torment for children. It makes me think about my own life experience and what lies behind the one talent that I have discovered in myself, that is the ability to read dreams, and how it came about as the result of falling in love with Melanie Klein and approaching her like an arrow from the bow, determined to have analysis with her. Not a matter of desire—a matter of life and death. It is an interesting story; I was in the United States Air Force at that time and had spent several years lying and scheming to be stationed in Great Britain in order to undertake analysis with her. As I stepped on to the plane to come to the United Kingdom, I got a change of orders, shifting me to Germany. By the time I reached Germany, I was dying of pneumonia, but also murderous, absolutely murderous, and I only remember getting on the telephone and screaming that I would murder somebody if they didn't shift me back to the UK. I woke up the next morning on the boat from the Hook of Holland, and started my analysis with Mrs Klein the next day. I would have killed somebody—there is no doubt.

That's not the same as discovering something. But it is certainly not an invention—you don't *invent* that you will kill somebody if you don't get your way. There are times when it is so factual that it is not possible to consider it an invention. The analysis with Mrs Klein changed my life. It changed me from a nice American boy to a nasty piece of work. But it was a great relief knowing this fellow that my parents had thought was so nice. And when Mrs Klein wrote a book about my envy, I was thrilled. Now that transformation from being a baseball-playing American boy to being a nasty piece of work released the possibility of my actually learning to read.

It was my mother's heartache that I never read a book. My eldest sister read all the books in the house and they belonged to her. Finally, though, I did begin to learn to read, and discovered how marvellous books are, because through books one can discover one's identifications. To my Cupid's-arrow identification with Melanie Klein, I added a spouse for her, with the wonderful name of Darcy Wentworth Thompson, whose book *Growth and Form* had been a sort of Bible for me during my undergraduate years. This man was the epitome of the naturalist, studying nature and filled with wonder at the miracles of nature, and it was thrilling. Then I discovered people like Gregor Mendelaev, with his periodic table, still for me a miracle. These real discoverers are very much associated for me with the few lines of poetry that have stuck in my head. Like "Did he who made the Lamb make thee?" Yes. Or, . . . Nor ever chaste except thou ravish me"—Donne's marvellous poem. I just finished a lovely book called *The Shadow of Cervantes* by Wyndham Lewis. Such a nice man. Well, along with Darcy Wentworth Thompson, I also discovered Alfred North Whitehead, who is for me the exemplar of a man who used language to discover things, while developing a unique language of his own for describing the world as he met it. He called this kind of discovering "an adventure"; and it was an adventure. It was lovely to read this book of his, to see the world unfolding before you like a flower.

Well, this is one of the benefits of ageing: I discover that reading is endless; there are so many people who write well. I'm not one of them; it is not my talent. But I can tell a good story if a patient will dream it for me.

The problem of spirituality, as it has begun to sort itself out in my mind, is connected with a family culture. There was nothing special about my family culture. Except that my parents were so special, and I deceived them into thinking that I was a nice baseball-playing boy; it is true that that was all I seemed to care about—horses, and playing. I certainly didn't enjoy school until about age ten or eleven. It didn't occur to me to enjoy school. I can regret now the opportunities I wasted. But they didn't appear as opportunities, they just appeared as variations of boredom. It didn't occur to me—is all that can be said about it. I didn't begin to get an education until I began to read.

Now, as far as the application of this to psychoanalysis is concerned: it seems to me absolutely essential that we concentrate on discovering, and do not yield to the temptation to invent. In Philip Pullman's wonderful trilogy, *His Dark Materials*, his little heroine Lyra learns that her survival has been purely the consequence of her being a liar; and she agrees with the harpy that screams at her "liar, liar, liar!" Are Philip Pullman's books full of inventions? No, I think they are full of discoveries. The great discovery, as far as I can see, is in *The Amber Spyglass*, which has to do with how the dust of consciousness is running out, because Will with his "subtle knife" opened windows between the different worlds but didn't close them, so the dust of consciousness just ran out of these windows. It seems to me to be a piece of optimism, at the end of the book, that Will has to dedicate his life to going back and closing all the windows that he left open. And it parallels the other part of this story: that Lyra has to be a reincarnation of Eve, and to refuse the apple. Well—I don't know if that was a good thing or a bad thing. But it certainly is a very imaginative trilogy. It was such a pleasure to read, and so full of optimism. Now whether it is a spiritual book . . . it is delicately balanced between invention and discovery. One would be inclined to say there is no possibility of believing in it; but there is also no possibility of not believing in it.

"Except thou ravish me . . ." That couples with the Shakespeare sonnet, which I can never remember. . . "The expense of spirit in a waste of shame / Is lust in action". What a nice audience. Thank you.

RESPONSE BY DAVID MAYERS

Every time I meet Dr Meltzer, in person or in writing, I come away with lots to be grateful for. This morning I have his lovely expression "miracle-perceptive", which captures exactly the essence of what I want to talk about. I start with an apparent impasse, and then try to describe a way of avoiding it. The impasse is this: if someone talks to me of, for instance, Christian, Islamic, or Jewish spirituality I find no problem in knowing what they mean; since in each case there is a defined object of worship, and spirituality is about developing a relationship with that object. (Why anyone should believe in such an object is another question.) If the notion of spirituality is taken outside such a context, I begin to have problems. There are certain concepts: awe, reverence, holiness, miracles, wonder, mortality, and death, which are essential in exploring certain aspects of our world; and if that's what spirituality means, fine. But I think that quite a lot of people want to take things further than that, to claim that somehow, however nebulously, there must be some sort of world mind, outside ourselves, because nothing can be made sense of otherwise. And I have to say that I see such a claim as an omnipotent, wish-fulfilling phantasy, whose function is to avoid the pain of having to acknowledge I just don't know what to say here. Scientists such as Richard Dawkins or Steve Jones have been eloquent in expounding how marvellous the structure of the world is; how fascinating, for instance, is the mathematics that we need to describe, and then further to explore, the minutiae of the universe. Psychoanalysis is equally awe-inspiring in making it possible to describe aspects of the psyche. (I think especially of Klein's elaboration of the depressive position and of Dr Meltzer's work on the aesthetic perspective.) What more can one want? Of course, there are times when we don't know how to proceed (yet). But to deal with the frustration of inadequate descriptive tools by throwing up a pseudo-explanation seems to me to be a perverse sort of dishonesty. Certainly those who think they can justify their appeal to some thinking power beyond ourselves will disagree; and I want to find a way not be drawn into a sterile ping-pong match sort of argument. So let me find another starting place.

When Kant was thinking about the sense of awe with which we meet the sublime, he offered, as examples, the starry heavens above, and the moral law within. This is a very fruitful pairing, partly because it claims the moral law within as a natural phenomenon, not, as many wish to claim, a purely cultural one. Now Kant's account of moral law is rather cerebral and emotionally unsatisfying. But there is a tradition, dating at least from Plato and Aristotle, which tries to describe, and thus to expand the sense of, what it means to live a good life: in terms of what are known as the cardinal virtues—justice, temperance, courage, and practical wisdom. It is a curious thing that in psychoanalysis justice and temperance have been rather thoroughly explored by a negative road. We know a great deal—partly due to Dr Meltzer's work—about greed and envy: in as far as greedy and envious impulses can be held at bay, then we move towards justice and temperance. (It's striking that in the paranoid–schizoid position very strange things happen to the virtues: think how, when the Victorians spoke of temperance, they limited its meaning to not drinking any alcohol, and forgot about more general moderation—surely a very paranoid thought.) I'm not going to talk further about justice and temperance—that's been done in its own way.

Courage and practical wisdom haven't been examined nearly so thoroughly in psychoanalytic circles: though Dr Meltzer has long spoken of the importance of introducing our patients to the notion of courage—and it takes a lot of courage to face up to our own nastiness. So I'm going to talk about my work with a patient whose therapy made me think about his learning to exercise these virtues.

When his therapy began, he talked at length about his very imaginative, creative father who was, when frustrated, absolutely incontinent, bursting into violent rages; and he was often frustrated, feeling that the world did not appreciate his work. And about his mother, who was either sweetly, saintly passive, mourning the awfulness of the world in a quite ineffective way; or was slobbily, disgustingly passive, eternally eating chocolate while watching television, having a disgusting kitchen where everything was sticky. There was also a horrid younger brother who was dirty, sullen, rude, and untidy: so that what could you do but hit him whenever you got the chance? And a cousin, who was fortunate in that his father left shortly after he was born: so that he had a beautiful, alluring, sexy mother all to himself. The combination of the oedipal and the violent was very striking.

At the beginning his dreams were often set in what became known as the shit-kitchen: this because of a dream where he was in an underground kitchen inhabited by a tribe of cannibal brothers who drank each others' blood and ate mother's shit; my patient was too frightened to join in but unable to leave. (Those familiar with Dr Meltzer's work on anal masturbation and claustrophobia may imagine how much he helped me to understand this material.) As my patient became aware of his own violence and grandiosity, via a realization of how horrible he'd been to his brother and how ill he'd made his mother by being so, he came out of the shit-kitchen—though whenever he got too frightened he ran, in his dreams, back into it. What took its place was a house on Hampstead Heath, potentially quite a beautiful house, but made threatening by a gang of intimidating, filthy tramps, who camped outside the garden fence in a way that made anyone entering or leaving the house run the gauntlet through them. The tramp dreams were a vehicle for him to sort out his own violence and unpleasantness from his father's and brother's, his fear and timidity from his mother's; and to understand something of how he determinedly put such qualities outside himself with the result that since violence and creativity were so mixed up, his own creative qualities were denied or inhibited. Then his dreams were often set in the streets of his university town. He would dream of walking along the top of a building, high in the air and about to fall; or of cycling in a wobbly, unsteady way along the street. Various representations of me appeared ready to help him keep his balance, but he was so frightened and ashamed that when the helping figure appeared he would run away and hide. At the same time, there were dreams featuring two colleges, neither of which he had attended but which were named, respectively, after him and his mother; he dreamed of speculating about the relationships between members of the colleges. His mother began to emerge as a much more credible and dimensioned woman, whose thinking had made a positive impact on him. But he remained, in the dreams, outside the buildings.

In the final session of his therapy he brought this dream: he was coming to see me, for lunch, in my college which was strange to him. He entered the grounds and saw a building that was like a Greek tomb: he thought it beautiful, but was sad because it reminded him that I would die. He had lunch with me and felt welcome, but was suffused with the feeling that he was a visitor, that it was not his place, that he would have to leave. He left me, and walked sadly towards the station, down a street lined with small terraced houses. He saw a house which had been for sale but was now marked as sold: and realized that it was his house, in which he was going to live with his father. It was empty, so he would be able to choose his own furniture.

I thought that his scaling down from the grandiosity of college to the little house, but realizing that he could furnish it himself, was an act of great courage and achievement. It was striking, though, that he was going to live with his father. And I did wonder what had happened to mother? So that I was not surprised when two years or so later, he asked to come back just once a week. He concentrated on thinking about ways in which father, mother and son could make a life together, and went away with a more established idea of a positive family life. His need to find a capacity for courage in himself was obvious: not so much courage to face a raging father, the shit-kitchen and, the tramps, but the courage to acknowledge how difficult he found it to know about his vulnerability and his need for help.

A personal journey through psychotherapy and religion

Christopher MacKenna

Introduction

Some years ago I was one of a number of psychotherapy colleagues who met for a day to talk about spirituality. We gathered cheerfully but left deeply shocked, wounded by the violent feelings that the topic had aroused. At the meeting we discovered that we all had strong, but very diverse, spiritualities, for which we lacked a common language. Coming from different religious and non-religious backgrounds we struggled to articulate our most precious intimations about life, but found them sounding strangely insubstantial. Then, perhaps because psychotherapy was the one thing we knew we had in common, we began translating each other's experience into psychological language. We all found this infuriating. Psychological language did not have the same resonance, for us, as our private spiritual languages; and we lacked the personal information about each other that would have made adequate translation possible.

Reflecting on this experience, I found myself wondering what we had hoped to achieve by meeting. We had been drawn by the word spirituality, but without an agreed understanding of its meaning. We tried to articulate our core values, and touched on some fundamental issues: love, sexuality, death, and god. To some extent we shared our pathology; but we could not leave it there because we had such powerful associations to each other's language. Religious words sparked conflict and aggression in those whose struggle had been to attain selfhood through separation from religious entrapment. When someone spoke of the death of god[1] as the moment when they came alive, this hurt people for whom god was still a source of life.

Was the venture misconceived? Should we have remained colleagues, supporting each other in professional ways but maintaining a discrete distance? That would have been safe, but something was driving us on. Looking back, I think that "something" was our awareness that psychotherapeutic training had changed us, giving us new ways of looking at the world but also, painfully, sometimes alienating us from friends, family, and co-religionists who could not comprehend our novel point of view. Perhaps, when we agreed to meet, we were more desperate than we realized. I think this lonely and disturbing experience is quite widely shared within the psychotherapeutic community, but is seldom addressed in professional meetings, which often seem strangely reticent to acknowledge either the metaphysical or the existential implications of our work.

Of course, analytic thinking has long been preoccupied with the subject of religion and there are now finely nuanced analytic studies which go way beyond Freud's ground-breaking attempts to get a handle on this puzzling phenomenon. I am particularly grateful for the contributions of Rizzuto (1979, 1998), Meissner (1984, 1987, 1992), and Jung (*Collected Works*). Rizzuto has written extensively about the formation and transformation of our images of God. She believes that each of us has an internal image of the god in whom we do, or do not, believe; and that this image is, consciously and unconsciously, a potent force within our inner worlds. She offers empirical research and rich case histories illuminated by clear theoretical formulations, but she never seems to wonder about the metaphysics of the analytic process itself, which seem to me to subvert the rather rationalistic assumptions implicit in many accounts of analytic work. One surprising discovery of my own journey through faith and analysis has been the way in which analytic experience has revived my confidence in what used to be called the "supernatural".

Meissner is a Jesuit priest who has worked as a clinical professor of psychiatry at Harvard Medical School and as a Training and Supervising Analyst at the Boston Psychoanalytic Institute. In his opinion, psychoanalysis can say nothing about the ultimate truth or falsity of Christian belief (a comment often made by Jung), but it can make observations about the psychological structures and dynamics involved in believing. Accordingly, he receives the faith as taught by the Roman Catholic Church and lays it side by side with his psychoanalytic knowledge. This means that psychoanalysis has to engage with a mature doctrinal expression of faith, rather than with its more infantile or pathological manifestations, but it leaves open huge questions about the genesis of that faith.

Jung offers a different approach to the psychology of Christian experience. His genius was to translate (and sometimes to invert) religious concepts into psychological language. So, for Jung, the Incarnation becomes the process by which the unconscious becomes conscious (Jung, 1976, p. 342). Instead of god redeeming us, we redeem god through our struggle consciously to integrate and transcend the opposites as they emerge from the unconscious (Jung 1954). I resonate to this, but my more benign experience of Christianity makes me more optimistic than Jung about its capacity to contain and transform emerging psychic contents. Also, I am less ready than Jung simply to abandon the objective, transcendent dimension of religious experience.

Rizzuto, Meissner and Jung offer important insights, but the fraught meeting with my colleagues convinces me that analytic theory has some way to go before it can engage adequately with the varieties of spiritual experience. Faced with such complicated and emotive issues there is always the temptation to stand back and try to deal with them at second hand, as if we could process them "out there"; but what distinguishes Freud's "Interpretation of dreams" (1900a) and Jung's *Memories, Dreams, Reflections* (1963) from the seminal documents of other psychological schools was their readiness to plumb the depths of their own experience. This is the primary research method available to depth psychologists. To my way of thinking, commitment to the analytic attitude is as much an act of faith as religious commitment, and our lives are the experimental field in which the value of each commitment is either proved or found wanting. If I am to say anything meaningful about my understanding of the relationship between psychotherapy and spirituality I will have to draw on my own experience, seeking to understand the ways in which my personal spirituality has grown out of cultural influences and developmental struggles, and the part which therapeutic experience has played in this process.

Some personal history

The idea of god entered my conscious world quite early on. I must have been about three when my mother explained that I had a guardian angel. The scene was my bedroom, and the context my reluctance to stay in bed, on the top floor of our narrow terraced house, while she went down to the basement to cook my father's supper. The idea intrigued me. "How close is the angel?" I asked. "Very close", she said, with the special emphasis she used when she wanted to be reassuring. I felt torn. An invisible angel was a poor substitute for my gorgeous-smelling mother, but I was curious. I let her tuck me up in bed and stayed there long enough to listen as her footsteps descended five flights of stairs to the basement. Then, quick as a flash, I was out of bed and whirling round with my pillow, trying to detect if I had made contact with any invisible object in the room. The experiment was inconclusive.

My mother taught me a prayer which began "Jesus, tender Shepherd, hear me', though I said "Jesus, Tender, Shepherd, hear me". Saying the prayer made me feel good because it pleased my mother, and life was more manageable when she was happy. Sitting in the bath though, aged about four, we got into a spat about the crucifixion. "Why didn't Jesus come down from the cross and slish his enemies?" I said, thinking of my wooden sword and what I would do to anyone who tried to crucify me. "He couldn't." "Why not?" I asked, thinking he must be pretty weak. If she had an answer I cannot remember it, but I do remember that, at some stage, she began to cry, and life became unbearable when she cried. I do not know what triggered my mother's tears, but I suspect that the contemptuous grandiosity with which I rejected Jesus' passivity was as much a defence against her depression as a response to the passion story. Later, that grandiosity would become a defence against the vulnerability and humanity of Christ—which is, for me, a way of saying the vulnerability of the human condition.

It seems that, through the internalization of these contrasting (and perhaps repeated) experiences with my mother, two very different complexes began to form in my inner world. The first was life enhancing: the idea of a god with whom I could enjoy play, and playful sexual activity. The second, somehow also associated with god, was deadly: an awful powerlessness, hovering over unthinkable depths of despair.

At eight I was sent to boarding school, and my universe split in two. There was much to enjoy, but the first terms were inward agony, the worst moment coming when I realized I had forgotten what my mother looked like. In retrospect I can understand that my rage obliterated her face: that is how I interpret the nightmares I had of my parents being held captive and tortured by sadistic criminals. At the same time I can now understand what I was then even more unconscious of: my terror of separation.

Outwardly stolid but inwardly wrecked, I picked up a book called *The House of Prayer* (Converse, 1935). It was about a small boy called Timothy, separated from his Mother and left in an unfamiliar place with his Grandfather; but Timothy's life changed, and he became more thoughtful about his inner states and actions, through meeting an angel. Together they made journeys, meeting children in different times and places. Timothy learned about the history of the church, about prayer and self-awareness, about life being bigger than his personal distress. Finally, all creation got caught up in a great act of worship in which the boundary between time and eternity dissolved.

Angels, Mother, separation, the mix was tailor-made for me. I became aware that it is possible to have an inner world that is bigger than the outer world of our confinement. The limits of that inner/ outer world were vague: but I was not asking intellectual questions, rather, I was finding a space for my heart. Chapel acquired new meaning. I liked the singing and the General Thanksgiving from the *Book of Common Prayer*, which I got by heart. Thinking how much I still enjoy those words, I am aware how easily prayers can be used defensively, becoming magical mantras that can be repeated, not just mindlessly, but as a means of preventing thought and feeling, or as a substitute for action. Mention of mantras, though, reminds me of the use of words in meditation, where the intention is to preoccupy one part of the mind so as to liberate another. Words can also be symbols for emerging psychic contents. There are complexities here which call for profound attention in our clinical work, as we try to understand the significance of religious activities which may be strange to us.

The House of Prayer helped to define a religious "space" inside me in which my two god complexes could function side by side. On the one hand, I recognize the omnipotent way in which I used Timothy and the angel to counter the gnawing pangs of homesickness: lying in bed at night, it gave me such comfort to think of their adventures. On the other hand, the places they visited and the people they met were real and credible. This intellectual knowledge gave me a sense of the power of religion to bind people together across language and time. God was nowhere defined in this, but was somehow the atmosphere which permeated the story, with its strong moral emphasis on truthfulness, honesty (as much with oneself as with other people), and courage. Very importantly for my religious and psychological development, *The House of Prayer* got me praying. Not just repeating "Jesus, tender Shepherd, hear me," or the General Thanksgiving, but pouring out my feelings to god. As I did this I became conscious of my "heart" speaking. I heard myself, *but I also felt heard*, and this was significant to me. Inwardly I was beginning to flourish, but tucked inside was a carefully concealed vein of grandiosity: I had discovered a secret world no one else seemed to know.

Public school, when it came, was more violent and philistine than preparatory school, but it possessed a stone-built chapel, like a church, to which I warmed. The chapel offered peace—inner space—and privacy. The walls of the chapel were panelled with memorials to old boys killed in two world wars. I gazed at them and registered their ages: many only five years older than myself. Their intangible presence merged with memories of Remembrance Sunday Services at prep school, where we were told that the cream of British youth had died in Flanders. We could play in freedom because of their sacrifice. Should need arise, we must be prepared to die so that our children could survive. The message went home. Memorials, poppies, prayers, and martial music fused with inner despair, rage, and self-hatred to produce beautiful fantasies of how sad everybody would be when I made the supreme sacrifice.

Into this world walked a Franciscan Friar, who came to preach a series of Lenten addresses. Brother Peter was definitely counter-cultural. He talked about Buckingham Palace Garden Parties and hop picking in Kent, of prostitutes in Cable Street where he lived, and Borstal boys with whom he worked. The Jesus he incarnated stood for radical humanism—revolutionary in the hierarchical world of public school. Listening to him, Christianity became something not other-worldly but this-worldly; not that he denied the other world, but he taught that its values meant nothing unless realized in the here and now. This was my first conscious lesson in incarnation.

In this new vision, goodness ceased to be a matter of rules and became something recognizable by its beauty. But the more beautiful it became the more ugly I felt because I was ashamed of my insides, not least my compulsive masturbation. The right response seemed to be to make my confession (not compulsory for Anglicans); an experience memorable because it was the first time I opened my heart to another human being. The priest was what I needed: kind and down to earth. Whereas I had dragged myself to church filled with shame, I now walked on air: the "worst" about me was known, and still I was accepted. I had approached the ordeal in a black-and-white state of mind but was bowled over by the experience of acceptance and simple, human understanding. The Bible speaks about *chesed* and *charis*, loving kindness and freely given unconditional love, words that acquired resonance through this experience and became part of my new vision of the beauty and humaneness of holiness. At the same time, I was given a rudimentary picture of growing-up being like a process of plaiting in which there would always be loose ends waiting to be brought in. The important thing was not to be frightened of the loose ends, but grateful for their potential—the beginnings of a developmental theory.

Having fallen in love with god, nothing less than total commitment felt adequate, so I planned to follow Brother Peter into the religious life. Not, though, into the extraverted Franciscans: I feared their harum-scarum existence would distract me from my (highly distorted) concept of the mystical journey. So, aged eighteen, I knocked on the door of the Benedictines; unconscious as much of my flight from adult responsibility, competition, sex, and likely academic failure, as of the grandiosity that made me shun ordinary human existence. Lurking beneath both, more darkly, was the lure of the supreme sacrifice: love and death are sometimes close together.

Saint Benedict is one of the church's great psychotherapists. He understood that emotional and spiritual growth requires an adequate container. His monks vow stability within the enclosure of the monastery, where they enjoy simple food and adequate sleep, while undertaking to work on personal transformation. The externals of the life are not harsh, but inwardly the ego is decentred as the monk learns obedience to a superior who considers the needs of the community before individual whims. Monks are admitted on the understanding that they truly seek god but what they find, most immediately, is a mixed bunch of eccentrics with whom they have to learn to live. Tensions, internal and external, rise while, for several hours each day, the monk pours out the petitions of the psalms: every conceivable human emotion passing through his lips. In this secure but monotonous environment there is little refuge from one's inner world. Instead of exotic spiritual flights, the monk—if he can stand it—has gradually to recognize and own the complexes that drive him. Confession, here, is not just a matter of listing transgressions of a rule, but of observing one's perverse inclinations and seeking to understand what drives them.

In the monastery I found the security I lacked and a readiness, in my superiors, to utilize talents I did not know I had. Socially and intellectually, I blossomed; life became good, but there were no mystical flights. Inevitably, sex began to stir and I began to feel lonely in a way I never had before. With this came the fear that I might die before I had lived. Terrified of losing my sanctuary in the cloister I secretly redoubled my fasting. After four and a half years I left the community with an anorexic-style breakdown. I had yet to learn that god cannot be found at the cost of our true selves.

At this stage, nothing inward was resolved. As best I could I cobbled myself together and embarked on a university career. In almost every way, university was paradise—I met my wife!—but intellectual life at that time was still dominated by logical positivism. In his book *Confessions of a Philosopher* Bryan Magee calls it "intellectual terrorism" (Magee, 1997, p. 45), which ripped the heart out of religious propositions; and the psychologists were more interested in quantifiable experiments than in the human soul. I grew up, but left the university with deeper questions than when I started.

It was at this rather fraught moment that I first encountered the analytic world through membership of a case discussion group, led by a psychoanalyst and group analyst called Oliver Lythe. To this day the group remains my most intense group analytic experience, the extraordinary thing about it being the way in which the spontaneously emerging case was found, in different ways, to mirror the underlying dynamics of the group. From the perspective of the logical positivists, Lythe's interpretations—he confined his interventions almost completely to analysing the transference between himself and the group—were clearly nonsensical, and yet they evidently spoke to a shared dimension of our experience. We may have been eight individuals, but there was a collective dimension to our experience that startled and puzzled me. Repeatedly I found myself wondering, am I a "me"? Or are we a "we"? Are we eight discrete individuals? Or are we, in some way, linked, so that we function as parts of a greater whole?

Under the influence of this group and now avidly reading Freud and Jung, I found myself beginning to reinhabit a world that I had feared lost to me. Their understandings of symbolism and unconscious processes took me back to the medieval thought-world of the monastery, making me realize how rationalistic and "asymmetrical", in Matte Blanco's language, (Matte Blanco, 1998) much modern theological writing had become. To the logic-obsessed theologians of the 1960s, if something was "this" it could not also be "that", whereas religious imagery gains its force precisely from such symmetry where one and the same being can be virgin and mother, God and man, righteous and sinful, three and one, transcendent and immanent.

Finally, overwhelmed by my own neediness, I entered therapy. In the early months I dreamed constantly of wandering through monastic ruins. I did not know where I was, possibly Fountains, or Tintern, or Rievaulx. No one was about, just me with the stones and the grass and the empty tracery of the windows silhouetted against the sky. I had no sense of where I had come from or why I was there. My feelings were as barren as the sky: nothing I could get hold of. It took years, and a second analysis, finally to penetrate the schizoid core into which I had withdrawn in early life; but something began to stir inside me because, after some weeks, the dreams changed, and crowds of men, women, and children began to invade the ruined cloisters, all dancing. My religion was coming down to earth: why seek god in the heavens when his image can be found in every man and woman? But paradoxically, I was now entering a world, the world of depth psychology, that soon began to feel as mysterious as the mystical texts over which I had poured in the monastery.

Metaphysics

Oliver Lythe's case discussion group had raised the question, am I a "me"? Or are we a "we"? That question, and the disturbing possibilities it raised, stayed with me through years of analysis and training. In time I came across Freud's 1915 paper 'The unconscious', in which he comments,

> It is a very remarkable thing that the *Unconscious* of one human being can react upon that of another, without passing through the *Conscious*. This deserves closer investigation, especially with a view to finding out whether preconscious activity can be excluded as playing a part in it; but, descriptively speaking, the fact is incontestable. [Freud 1915e, p. 194]

That is an extraordinary assertion. If true, it has far reaching metaphysical consequences that undermine any simple, materialistic account of human existence. And yet my therapeutic experience supports Freud's concept of unconscious communication. Illustrations are inevitably anecdotal, but two early analytic experiences stuck firmly in my mind.

In the first case I was working with a violent and impulse-driven patient, with a rather borderline personality structure, who was becoming increasingly suicidal. After every session he would tell me that he had been to sit at the top of a multi-storey car-park, thinking how easy it would be to step into thin air. I was almost paralysed by anxiety about him until, in supervision, I finally managed to process some of the unthinkable material which I had been containing. Feeling greatly relieved I rushed back to the next session, ready to impart my new found wisdom, only to find that my patient came to the session having apparently already processed my discovery. The experience was both disconcerting and relieving.

Again, working with another borderline patient—an erratic attender at sessions—I found I could anticipate his arrival by the feelings of sick dread which possessed me a couple of minutes before he rang the bell. This experience was innocently confirmed, in relation to the same patient, by a conversation with a third party who knew my patient but did not (at least consciously) know that we were working together. This person had been so disturbed by similar feelings experienced in advance of unexpected visits from my patient that he had sought me out, knowing I was a psychotherapist, to consult me about them; a delicate situation.

Apart from Jung and some of his followers, depth psychologists have been strangely reluctant to follow up even the tentative suggestions made by Freud in his paper on "Dreams and occultism", in which he gave his opinion that "the scales weigh in favour of thought-transference" (Freud, 1933a: p. 54). When we speak of "unconscious communication," what do we mean? What is the medium by which unconscious communication takes place? The question is worth pressing because, if communication really is possible via the unconscious, this would suggest that we exist in the psyche, rather than psyche existing, separately, within each one of us. A. N. Whitehead is reputed to have said that the western philosophical tradition represents no more than footnotes to Plato. In a similar way, these thoughts about the unconscious bring us back to very ancient intuitions, to ideas of a world soul, or to St Paul who was happy to cite a pagan poet who said, "In god we live and move and have our being, for we too are his offspring" (Acts xvii, 28).

R. D. Hinshelwood is one psychoanalyst who has not been frightened to think about these issues. In *Therapy or Coercion?* he gives detailed material from psychoanalytic work and other settings to raise the question of whether a divided mind—he is thinking particularly of phenomena occurring in the most primitive forms of splitting, projection, and introjection—"can be encompassed in the ordinary metaphysical assumptions that govern other psychologies" (Hinshelwood, 1997: p. 115). As he says,

> Many . . . parts of the mind can disappear from a person through splitting and can then be re-found in another person as a result of the action of projection and introjection. [Hinshelwood, 1997, p. 179]

And again,

> If these are valid phenomena, then the common-sense metaphysical assumptions and claims about the unity of the mind and of the person have to change. [Hinshelwood, 1997, p. 181]

The subversive effect of analytic work on materialist assumptions about the nature of reality should come as no surprise to us. In his paper *Psycho-analysis and Telepathy*, originally read to Jones, Abraham, Eitington, Ferenczi, Rank, and Sacks in August 1921, but only published posthumously, Freud says:

> There is little doubt that if attention is directed to occult phenomena the outcome will very soon be that the occurrence of a number of them will be confirmed. [Freud, 1933a, p. 179]

My sense is that the existence of such anomalous events is not infrequently recognized in supervision but seldom talked or thought about in any systematic way. Two signal exceptions to this generalization are the collections of papers edited by Devereux (1953), and Totton (2003) that explore the occurrence of paranormal phenomena in psychotherapeutic situations in some detail. The effect of these papers is to reinforce my belief in the strange properties of psyche, and to make me wonder at the psychoanalytic community's reluctance to follow the leads offered by Freud and Jung.

Concluding thoughts

I have tried to describe some of the ways in which religious imagery and experience have become entwined in my life, and the way in which analytic experience has enlarged my metaphysical horizons. It took me a long time to accept the basic Christian insight, that there is no union with god that avoids the flesh, no world "beyond" that can be reached by despising or avoiding this world. Through my struggles I have come to realize that, for me, the essence of spirituality, what keeps me alive, is the capacity to preserve an inner space in which meaningful intercourse can happen, a space in which my continually evolving picture of god can be present, or absent. My faith and my analytic experience suggest that that intercourse can happen in different ways and at different levels, including the levels of mind and spirit; and that these levels are more extensive than the individual body.

But what of god? Coleridge, struggling to understand whether love "is the pursuit of a shadow, a self-created illusion . . . or if it is a beautiful Platonic reality, a projected form of the 'dear embodied Good' which really exists in its own being, in others and in Eternity" (Coleridge, 1996, p. 325), wrote a haunting poem, the title of which reads like a startling anticipation of psychoanalytic theory: "Constancy to an Ideal Object".

> . . . And art thou nothing? Such thou art, as when
> The woodsman winding westward up the glen
> At wintry dawn . . .
> Sees full before him, gliding without tread,
> An image with a glory round its head;
> So the enamoured rustic worships its fair hues,
> Nor knows he makes the shadow he pursues!
> [Coleridge, 1996, p. 192]

Is god simply an internal object? Do I make the shadow I pursue? In one sense yes, of course, I do; but is this—as the analytic world tends to believe—the whole story? I do not think so, and it is my therapeutic as much as my religious experience that makes me question the positivistic assumptions at the heart of so much analytic writing on therapy and religion.

Note

Although I believe in the objective reality of god I write "god" without a capital to remind myself that every statement about god is a human invention.

References

Coleridge, S. T. (1996). *Selected Poems*. R. Holmes (Ed.). London: Penguin.

Converse, F. (1935). *The House of Prayer*. London: JM Dent & Sons.

Devereux, G. (Ed.) (1953). *Psychoanalysis and the Occult*. New York: International Universities Press.

Freud, S. (1900a). The interpretation of dreams. *S.E.*, *1V* & *V*. London. Hogarth.

Freud, S. (1915e). The unconscious. *S.E.*, *X1V*. London. Hogarth.

Freud, S. (1933a). *New Introductory Lectures on Psycho-Analysis*. *S.E.*, *XX11*. London: Hogarth.

Hinshelwood, R. D., (1997). *Therapy or Coercion*. London: Karnac.

Jung, C. G., (1954). *Answer to Job*, *C.W.*, *X1*. London: Routledge and Kegan Paul.

Jung, C. G., (1963). *Memories, Dreams, Reflections*. London. Collins and Routledge and Kegan Paul.

Jung, C. G., (1976). *C. G. Jung: Letters, vol. ii 1951–1961*. Selected and edited by G. Adler and A. Jaffé. London: Routledge & Kegan Paul.

Magee, B. (1997). *Confessions of a Philosopher*. London. Weidenfeld and Nicholson.

Matte Blanco, I. (1998). *The Unconscious as Infinite Sets: An Essay in Bi-logic*. London: Karnac.

Meissner, W. W. (1984). *Psychoanalysis and Religious Experience*. New Haven, NJ: Yale University Press..

Meissner, W. W. (1987). *Life and Faith: Psychological Perspectives on Religious Experience*. Washington, DC: Georgetown University Press.

Meissner, W. W., (1992). *Ignatius of Loyola: The Psychology of a Saint*. New Haven, NJ: Yale University Press.

Rizzuto, A-M. (1979). *The Birth of the Living God: A Psychoanalytic Study*. Chicago, IL: University of Chicago Press.

Rizzuto, A.-M. (1998). *Why did Freud Reject God? A Psychodynamic Interpretation*. New Haven, NJ: Yale University Press.

Totton, N. (Ed.), (2003). *Psychoanalysis and the Paranormal: Lands of Darkness*. London: Karnac.

RESPONSE BY BERNARDINE BISHOP

C hris MacKenna's first story—about the meeting where the participants discussed their spirituality and felt, as the day went on, wounded and outraged—is very telling. "At the meeting," he says, "what we seemed to be trying to do was to find a way of articulating our core values, the things we believed in and held on to when everything else was falling apart, the things which made life meaningful for us, the things which got us out of bed in the morning, that saved us from despair." We are defensive, presumably, about such deep and personal things because we don't know where we would be without them. But as his paper goes on, we see that he tries to name these deep things, to explore and analyse their nature, to see where they come from in him, within and without; and that nothing does, actually, crumble, but remains strong, tried and tested, rather than undermined, by the process of being thought about.

This is the first lecture in our Psychotherapy and Spirituality series in which the speaker has said: "I believe in God". I think this is rather brave of Chris. Why should it be a difficult and a courageous thing to say? There are many bygone centuries in which it would not have been a brave thing to say and many parts of the world today where it still wouldn't be. Quite the contrary. But this is the twenty-first century, and we are in London, and at a psycho-analytic psychotherapy institution.

So much negativity is projected on to that statement. Because of where we are, culturally, in space and time, it conjures up so much more than it asserts: images of respectability, rigidity, bondage to tradition, naïvety, unexamined mind-sets, bigotry, smug delusion, and anti-symbolic thinking . . . not to mention well-meaning people at the front door with tracts in their hands; sex as sin. None of these necessarily belongs, but there it is. Because of what is projected into the statement, the person hearing it may glaze over, smile politely, and begin to edge away. The person making the statement may know about these projections. He may share them. That's what makes it a brave thing to say.

What Chris MacKenna has been talking to us about this morning is at the opposite pole from this projection. It has been tremendously alive, and has offered no foregone conclusions. No conclusion at all, in fact. The movement of his paper is all about process and becom-ing, hints and possibilities. And yet he can say, unblushingly, the first of eight speakers on this subject to do so: "I believe in God". He also said: I love and trust God. To be exact with the quote: "I find it easier to love and trust God than Jung did", which runs just as counter to the therapeutic culture. But not open in quite the same way to negative projections. Not so liable to be heard as an empty cliché. More unsaturated language, Bion might say.

The word "belief" is commonly used in either of two very differ-ent senses. There is belief as in: I believe in you. And there is belief as in: I believe in nitrogen. Or Mount Everest. The first use of the word is charged with feeling. The second assents to something that may be of no emotional significance, though it is presumed to exist. Nitrogen and Everest. If the "I believe in God" is heard as the second use of the word, as acceptance of a fact of a fixed and exter-nal sort, it is very different from being taken to imply—as in "I believe in you"—a positive relationship, a strong emotional dynamic, a conviction of the heart.

Chris shows us in his paper how "I believe in God" can be like the "I believe in you" sort of statement, and in that context the love and trust find their places quite naturally. In this sense "I believe" means I love and I trust, much more than it means "I give mental assent to the existence of . . ."

This reminds me of Karen Armstrong raising a chuckle a few months ago in this room when she said how heartily sick and bored she gets of being asked: do you believe in God? I think we felt that what she found so unwelcome and so unanswerable was a question put in the nitrogen register, which only had an interesting meaning for her in the other.

In telling us, as he has, about the early development of his faith, Chris is not talking about belief in God as in nitrogen. The belief has been a living and growing relationship, characterized by fidelity despite change; by experience, bitter and otherwise, and learning from it; by facing and embracing uncertainty; by enduring loss of known and comfortable positions. Chris has also said that he is a Christian. And that's another brave thing to say, in our climate. Again, it is a statement that is likely to be heavily and negatively projected into, and, in saying it, he takes that risk. It is interesting, though I don't know where this thought could go, that both Christianity and psychoanalysis spring from Jewish roots.

Chris MacKenna introduces us to Ana-Maria Rizzuto and William Meissner—he introduces me, in any case—and then talks about Jung's explorations of the links between psychotherapy and religion. All these interest him, and become interesting in his hands for us. But he doesn't find in them the expression of the beauty most ancient and most new that he wants to share with us, and he tries to get closer to that in a very personal account of his life—childhood, adolescence, adulthood. We can glimpse how the early years played on the later, and we can be very grateful indeed to him, I think, for being so open and honest. This part of the paper is rich with images and dreams, and with intriguing personalities and situations, and with pain, and growth, and insight.

We then get to a section of the paper where Chris MacKenna discusses puzzling events that sometimes happen in psychotherapy. There is the suicidal patient whose persecution is lessened at the same time as Chris, his therapist, finally processes some of his own persecutory anxiety in supervision. Then there is the mutual acquaintance of Chris and a dread-provoking patient, who unwittingly is drawn to consult Chris about the dread this man provoked in him, not knowing Chris was his therapist. Third, there is the patient who leaves a very important session expecting retribution from her mother and has a car crash.

Personally, I would feel willing to accept the second of these three vignettes as coincidence—the small world phenomenon. The first and the third I am happy to have exemplify the extraordinary strength of unconscious processes: in the first case, processes we know of as projective identification; in the third, an extreme manifestation of the way in which the unconscious, more in some people than others, continually sculpts symbolic events out of ordinary life. There are many great wonders here, but I don't myself feel helped with them by any of the ESP range of explanations.

These events take me back to the dialectic between Nathan Field and Jennifer Silverstone: do we or do we not need to invoke more than the things we continue to discover clinically about the nature of relationship, in order to think about these not infrequent consulting-room phenomena? In a broadbrush—and possibly very irritating—way, I feel Jungians go one way on this sort of thing, and the psychoanalytic tradition the other. Perhaps it is to forestall this irritation that Chris recruits both Freud and, more startlingly, Bob Hinshelwood on the side of the occult.

But let me not lose where Chris MacKenna's thought is actually going at this point. He is suggesting that contact of unconsciouses—paranormal or natural, whichever—throws light on the question about whether I am an "I" or whether I am a "we". The question is: "whether we exist in the psyche, rather than the psyche existing, separately, in each one of us." Chris cites Plato and St Paul. He could have mentioned Paul's notion of us as the mystical body of Christ; but he didn't. Also perhaps Bion, and thoughts about an existence prior to the thinker in whom they find themselves. So Chris was spare here. I flag up this point in the paper as an important one in the hope that it won't get lost to the discussion.

Chris's final point is about whether narcissism is the collective neurosis of the psychotherapeutic world: ". . . reluctant to conceive a source of life beyond our control," he asks, "dare we receive anything that we have not invented?" This is a trenchant and paradoxical challenge. Do we, as therapists, deny the existence of a God external to self out of pathological pseudo-self-sufficiency? We to whom, as a profession, trustful dependence on an external object is a paradigm so important to our conception of transference and of the development of personality?

I think most psychoanalytic psychotherapists are pretty sure that man has invented God. Collectively, that would be where the profession stands. Chris is saying that his internal world and experience tell him something else. In laying his cards on the table, Chris MacKenna has offered us something about as fundamental as it could be for us to think about.

What happens *between* people

Josephine Klein

M y title, "What happens *between* people?" is intended to draw attention to a gap in our common language by means of which we talk about what happens when people affect one another. We all have theories about this, but no common language for comparing our theories. For instance, we tend to talk as though there were clear boundaries between people: "I am Jo; you are Jim". Winnicott writes of a "limiting membrane" between one person and another (1958, p. 239; 1965, p. 148), but while this is a useful metaphor, there is in fact no membrane separating my mind from Jim's—nothing analogous to the skin that visibly maintains our separate identities. How can we talk about this to one another?

I propose to take from algebra's "set theory" a trick called a *Venn diagram* (Allwein & Barwise, 1996). Venn diagrams allow us to draw lines round sets of items that share a particular something. Thus, I can draw a line, for instance, around everything I think of as "not-I", and I can draw lines around everything I think of as "not I", and one can draw lines around everything I think of as "you", and another line around everything I think of as "not-you".

These boundary-lines are conventionally represented by circles. I can draw a circle that encloses all that "I" am, and another circle that encloses all that "you" are, floating in a universe that comprises "not I and not you".

You and I may meet and find we share certain things: "us" or "ours".

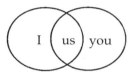

We now see a crescent-shaped area

enclosing what I am but not you, and another area

enclosing what you are but not I, and an area which is shared, in a narrow sense of what we have in common, or in a broad sense, what we can command between us:

Narrow sense   Broad sense

"Intersect" is a word for a process that both parties recognize when they say "we". Yet it can be one-sided: I may feel at one with my horse, or a mountainside, or a symphony, or something else ineffable whose nature I cannot fathom but with which I have experienced an encounter, and at-one-ness, a relatedness, while the horse or the mountain may not reciprocate this awareness. "Intersect" is, of course, a metaphor. Intersects may not exist in the same sense in which Oxford Street exists—or they may—but I take the view that some intersects are realms to which "Highest", "Deepest", "Beyond", "Within", and other such spacial terms for the ineffable may apply. Hence one person's Highest may be another person's Deepest or Within. Now to apply this to some more familiar ideas.

Jungian, Freudian, and Kleinian traditions on common ground

The concept of a common ground of mental processes—i.e. of an intersect—keeps appearing and disappearing in various forms in the history of psychotherapy. Some have speculated that all the mental processes of some people—or perhaps of all people—intersect; that is, are in communication, albeit perhaps unconsciously. In this realm people's minds are thought by some to meet or mingle with one another, and perhaps also with other entities, such as Archetypes, in a Collective Unconscious. Some of our motivation may originate in this realm. This common ground realm is thought by some to be where the processes of projective identification take place.

Hinshelwood on projective identification.

Hinshelwood explicitly denies that Melanie Klein believed in that kind of intersect. His *Dictionary of Kleinian Thought* (1989), after going through twenty pages scrupulously distinguishing and defining the uses to which the term "projective identification" has been put since the 1940s, he returns to Klein and insists that she did not believe that there is a condition in which the mental processes of patient and therapist meet and interact in ways other than those accounted for by perceptions of, and deductions from, subtle behavioural indications of the other's phantasy life. There is no intersect of the kind which would be created by a mental space equally occupied by two people, in which important transactions take place on a plane removed from what can be photographed. He cites Ogden (1979 and 1982) as maintaining a contrary view.

Hinshelwood returns several times to the distinction, exemplified by Betty Joseph's work (1975 and thereafter), that people may become aware of a thought or phantasy that seems to be their own but that they then realize that this same thought is the one the other person had been entertaining about *them.* This thought had not arisen from their own cogitations but had sprung from the impact of the other person's hints and behaviour. As Hinshelwood sees it, we do not have to believe in an interpersonal process, such as thought-transference, in a mental realm where that is possible—no intersect of that kind. Hinshelwood insists that Joseph is describing what the experience is like for her, subjectively, when she describes projective identification; she is not describing how the process works.

Some Jungian uses of the concept of intersects

I tend to regard religious experiences, in the first instance at least, as part of the "non-I" part of the Self entering or becoming known to the "I" part. They therefore connote for me a potential for further self-realization, further restoration of an original unity and in-touchness with oneself and with Reality. This entering may take the form of an implosion, a revelation, a breakthrough from the non-I into the I, or a personal, quasi-sexual mystical impregnation or union. [Redfearn, 1985, p. 48]

Redfearn must mean here that he has a Self, part of which is not-Redfearn, of which he is unconscious: it is Redfearn in an intersect that also holds something Other. Redfearn, typically of this school of thought, credits this Other with a kind of Reality that merits a capital initial. This reality is Redfearn's (or he is Its), but it is also other people's.

Nathan Field (1996) posits a rather similar realm where people may encounter one another, an intersect invested with reality, or at least with another, though not an "other" that merits Redfearn's capital initial. Field posits a Fourth Dimension, which can be experienced as "the simultaneous union and separation of self and other" that a Venn diagram can neatly picture. "I have in mind those moments when two people feel profoundly united with one another yet each retains an enriched sense of his or her own identity" (*ibid.*, p. 71). Field believes that without this dimension we are handicapped in our therapeutic endeavours. Writing that the Freudian positivistic approach "cannot reach the cold split off parts of us", he continues:

> The surgical probe of insight cannot melt this frozen core; it can be reached only by the therapist's own heart and soul, which is what Jung (1954) meant by "coniunctio"' and Bion called "at-one-ment". [Field, 1996, p. 142]

For many Jungians the ineffable intersect is a friendly realm "melting the cold split-off elements . . .". Clearly, some people can lose themselves in the experience and are very happy about it. But others feel a desolate nothingness or emptiness. The blurring of the accustomed boundaries to the familiar self may be differently experienced by people of different predispositions. Marcus West, in an unfortunately as yet unpublished lecture given to the Society of Analytical Psychology in 1999, considers an intersect of this kind to be a state that is incompatible with what he considers the ego, defined as the everyday self and the everyday assumptions by which we live. West is acutely sensitive to the pain such loss of ego may cause. He, and others like him, usefully counteract the sentimental assumption that everything in the universe would be fine if only we saw it in the right perspective.

Uncomfortable experiences in the ineffable intersect

It appears that different people have very different but equally genuine experiences in the intersect. Zaehner (1957, Chapter 5 and passim) has many references to what Jung called the "collective unconscious", positively or negatively experienced. So has William James in *Varieties of Religious Experience* (1902). Grotstein (1997) and

Eigen (1998) have written with respectful terror about ineffable experiences, in a style that suggests that they have personal knowledge of what they write about, a style that goes back to Luther and Calvin and beyond, to Isaiah and Ezekiel. They know the overwhelming power of the phenomena they describe; they feel an awe that transcends the usual facile assumption that what is greater than us must also be kinder, more moral, and describable in terms we can effortlessly understand. Both equate the great ineffable experiences with the powerful forces that erupt from some people's unconscious processes, and thus with what is diagnosed by more sedate minds as a psychotic breakthrough, but they are not reductionist about it.

Grotstein and Eigen feel supported in their views by their reading of W. R. Bion (how justly only an expert could determine). As Bion sees it, analyst and analysand endeavour to understand the operation of L (love), H (Hate), and K (Knowledge) and their opposites, in the analysand's mind. Somewhat apart from these, beyond K, stands O, Absolute Truth, Ultimate Reality. "O" is what Bion ultimately strives for in his work.

Grotstein (1997), in a detailed paper, elaborates on his understanding of the mystical elements in Bion's thoughts. He quotes:

> In the first stage [of group development] there is no real confrontation between the god and man because there is really no such distinction . . . In the second stage the infinite and transcendent god is confronted by man . . . In the third stage the individual—the mystic—needs to assert a direct experience of the god . . . The individuals show signs of their divine origins . . . [and] may be regarded as being incarnations of the deity; each individual retains an inalienable element which is part of the deity himself that resides in the individual. [Bion, 1970, p.77]

This quotation conveys the Jungian element in Bion well, but this is not what catches Grotstein's attention. Rather it is

> What Bion hints but fails to say—but I feel constrained to state it for him ... what Freud could not have stated—that ... "God" and the unconscious are the same phenomenon seen from different vertices. [Grotstein, 1977, p. 81]

and Grotstein goes on to argue that

O overreaches Heaven and hell in its ultra-majestic, paradoxical sweep . . . the experience of O may be dreadful like the sight of Sodom and Gomorrah, the Medusa, or Hades—or beatific and serene, depending in the vertex of emotional maturity and preparedness from which one approaches it. [Grotstein, 1977, p. 85]

If Grotstein is to be thought of as on the margin of the psychoanalytic canon, Eigen may be thought of a rather further out. But the useful contribution of these two is that they are writing with respect about phenomena shunned by more pin-striped psychoanalysts.

Eigen (1998) provides generous examples of his professional work with people visited by extraordinary experiences. Of necessity he works mainly not with joyous manic, but with the ones whose experiences are terrifying, who tell of encounters with thunderstorms, unshielded by Jehovah, and other soul-shaking events. It is difficult to determine whether Eigen sees these tremendous experiences as encounters with an Other: or as experiences in the collective unconscious: or more as an individual's personal realities, processed with either felicity or agony in unconscious ways: or, as the old theologians would have it, as encounters with a God or a devil distinctly "out there". Are we in a position to decide? Eigen clearly relates to his patients with admirable respect, and sustains them in their ordeals. He certainly seems of use to them, more use than I or other blander souls could be. He seems to keep them for years, and keeps validating for them that their experiences are worth respect.

Charles Williams and the world of images

Charles Williams takes intersects for granted, and his characters in his novels interact with each other and with symbols—he calls the Images—that resemble Jung's Archetypes and Plato's Ideas.

His is an elaborate imaginative system that illuminates his theology, his understanding of Dante's *Divine Comedy*, and his novels. For Williams, human identities and concepts do not have such impenetrable boundaries from one another as we usually attribute to them. And if people have not such impenetrable boundaries, then they can "stand in" for one another and for symbols. In

Many Dimensions (1931) the Lord Chief Justice also *is* Justice, i.e., there is an intersect containing Lord Darglay and the Archetype— the idea—of Justice. In several novels Williams has a character say "This is not Thou but Thou art this also", meaning both that a lion may be "Strength Personified", and that this strength may just as well be in Mr Jones or in some other phenomenon. In *Descent into Hell* (1937) Williams conveys in novel form one of his most important concepts, that of "co-inherence", which is almost his word for intersection. In this novel, the playwright Stanhope intersects in a very helpful way with a young woman, Pauline, who tells him she is terrified by a shadowy double she meets at unexpected moments. (Later we discover why: there is an intersect containing this Pauline and a long-dead ancestor waiting to be burnt at the stake. Pauline is carrying his fear for him, so that he is free of it, in the same way as Stanhope is offering to carry hers for her.)

> "I have a trick . . . of meeting an exact likeness of myself in the street
> . . . It comes from a long way off, and it comes up towards me, and
> I'm terrified—terrified—one day it'll come up and meet me . . . and
> then I shall go mad or die."
>
> "But," he said . . . "You have friends; haven't you asked one of them
> to carry your fear?"
>
> "Carry my fear?" she said . . . "How can anyone else carry your
> fear? Can anyone else see it and have to meet it?" . . .
>
> . . . "When you leave here you'll think of yourself that I've taken
> this particular trouble over, instead of you. You'd do as much for
> me if I needed it, or for anyone . . . It needs only the act. For what
> can be simpler than for you to think to yourself that I am there to
> be troubled instead of you, therefore you needn't be troubled—And
> what can be easier that for me to carry for a little while a burden
> that isn't mine?"

The intersect allows *substitution* and *exchange*, activities at the heart of Williams' view of life. Psychotherapists cannot fail to notice some resemblance between the processes Williams postulates and what goes on in the consulting-room, where distresses—as yet unmanageable by patients on their own—may be transformed by the therapist's containing and metabolizing responses.

Martin Buber's you-and me, I-and-that-thing-over-there.

Martin Buber based his psychology on two fundamental relationships conventionally translated as *I–Thou* and *I–It*. I think his views
are better understood in terms of the two fundamental experiences
"you-and-me" and *"I-and-that-thing-over-there"*.

> It is said that people experience their world. What does this mean?
> People travel on the surface of things and experience them . . . The
> world has no part in the experience. It permits itself to be experi-
> enced but it has no concern in this matter. [Buber, 1923, p. 3]

That is, there is no intersect.

> Every "it" has boundaries shared with other things. But when
> people say "you" they are not talking to a thing, they are not "talk-
> ing to" at all; they are relating to a person. [*ibid.*]

Once people are in this relationship, Buber maintains, there are
drastic alterations at the boundaries of their personalities. A new
creation comes into being:—a you-and-me, like Dr Doolittle's push-
mepullyou—an intersect. When you and I meet, we are both
changed. The only change that can happen in an "I-and-that-thing-
over-there" encounter—if encounter it can be called—happens in
my head, that narcissistic place.

It is just worth noting that some psychotherapists think and talk
about their own and their patients' unconscious processes as
though these were things: part-objects, important or unimportant
bits of personality. Other psychotherapists address their patients
more consistently as a personal being "thou" who may or may not
be conscious of some relevant aspects of himself or herself. This is
a more whole-object way of experiencing a person, more you-and-
me.

Buber wrestles to put into words a sense of affinity with nature:

> . . . that living wholeness and unity of the tree, which denies itself
> to the sharpest glance of the mere investigator. . . . discloses itself to
> the glance of one who says *Thou.* [Buber, 1923, p. 158]

Buber goes further! Still facing that tree he writes:

Our habits of thought make it difficult for us to see that here, awak-
ened by our attitude, something lights up and approaches us from
the source of being . . . and . . . we have to do justice to the reality
which discloses itself to us. [*ibid.*]

Almost, we can say hello to a tree and the tree will respond and
greet us. Buber appears here to be describing something very like
what psychotherapists at present imagine a small child's universe
to be like. The sense of contact and relationship may be in place and
working, even before the child has developed any intellectual
knowledge about the world as a realm "out there", as an "it". In a
very poetic passage that foreshadowed Winnicott, Buber writes
with a father's tenderness of the infant's experience at that stage, as
he imagines it:

The most primal nature of the effort to establish relation is already
to be seen in the earliest stage. . . . Timid glances move out into
indistinct space, towards something indefinite; and at times when
there seems to be no desire for nourishment, hands sketch delicately and dimly in the empty air, apparently aimlessly seeking and
reaching out to meet something indefinite. You may, if you wish,
call this animal action, but it is not thereby comprehended. For
these very glances will, after protracted attempts, settle on the red
carpet-pattern and not be moved until the soul of the red has
opened itself to them . . . [Buber, 1923, p. 42]

Harold Searles and Kenneth Wright on relatedness

Towards the end of the1940s, Harold Searles, recently out of the
army and later to become one of the great innovators of psychoanalytic psychotherapy, began to write *The Non-Human Environment in
Normal Development and Schizophrenia*. It was so counter to the spirit
of the time that no one could be found to publish it until 1960. The
opening sentences of his preface celebrate what the Catskill region
of the United States meant to him: "a beauty and an affirmation of
life's goodness", and "moments of deeply felt kinship with one's
non-human environment . . . to be counted among those moments
when one has drunk deepest of the whole of life's meaning".
Kinship and relatedness are keywords for this innovator in the
treatment of schizophrenic distress.

I believe that there is indeed one basic attitude which is of general validity, one central emotional orientation to which the mature human being returns vis-à-vis his non-human environment . . . *relatedness.*

By relatedness I mean, on the one hand, a sense of intimate kinship . . . on the other hand, a maintenance of our own sense of individuality . . . [Searles, 1960, p. 101]

Searles (1960, pp. 117ff) acknowledges his debt to Martin Buber and, in his own turn, Kenneth Wright was to acknowledge his debt to Searles, especially as regards the idea that, in nature and in art, we find ourselves moved by what Wright was to clarify as "forms answering to our subjectivity".

Some process exists by which we can reach out from ourselves towards what is outside ourselves and . . . if we are lucky, or if we are blessed, this may lead us to find a form answering to our own subjectivity. [Wright, 1996, p. 72]

Searles' revolutionary contribution to working with people afflicted by schizophrenic symptoms was his theory that he, the therapist, by being so familiar with his own madness, his own wish to destroy, burn down, swallow, merge, chew up, whatever, and by being *comfortable* with it, enabled his patients to recognize that he and they were alike, but that he was not terrified by what he was, nor driven into mad action by it. This recognition calmed his patients, and made them more able to contain themselves, because they could see that he contained much the same material. If he could, they could. He was the form answering to their subjectivity (Searles, 1979, Chapter 22; see also Klein, J., 1995, pp. 254–255).

The more we know ourselves, the more we are able to recognize others, declared Searles. There are some schools of thought that teach only the reverse of this process: that what we see in others, we then make our own—we see it in others first and only thereafter in ourselves. It is likely that both these processes operate at one time or another: sometimes introjection, sometimes projective identification, sometimes introjective identification, sometimes discovery, sometimes extractive identification (see Bollas, 1987, Chapter 9). The phrase "to see ourselves in others" covers all these possibilities and indeed, the early psychoanalytic use of the word "identification" did not distinguish between them.

Ogden's intersubjectivity, the analytic third

From the 1950s onwards in Britain, because of Donald Winnicott's influence (in the United States rather later) ideas began to be elaborated that allowed for an intersect where minds can meet and combine to create further thoughts and this had a benign influence on the practice of psychotherapy. This brief survey will end with a tribute to Winnicott, with his very English way of talking about complex matters. But we must first consider a first-rate mind of a very different bent: Thomas Ogden, representative of American precision and the use of a Graeco-Latinate style of writing. One of Ogden's starting points is Winnicott's famous dictum that "there is no such thing as a baby" (only a mother–baby entity), which Ogden re-tailors as:

> I believe that, in an analytic context, there is no such thing as an analysand apart from the relationship with the analyst, and no such thing as an analyst apart from the relationship with the analysand. [Ogden, 1994, p. 4]

and, on the same page, he writes of

> The experience of being simultaneously within and outside of the intersubjectivity of the analyst–analysand, which I will refer to as the "analytic third". [*ibid.*]

Tennis is just such an intersubjective experience. Unless people are playing, there is no such thing as tennis; when one participant walks off, tennis vanishes. Tennis is thus a "jointly constructed set of experiences" of the kind to which Ogden refers. It is created by its participants, as in psychotherapy, and in other kinds of encounter. In a later paper Ogden amplifies what he means by the "analytic third": it is another intersect phenomenon, another push-mepullyou:

> . . . the analytic third is not a single event experienced identically by two people; it is a jointly but asymmetrically constructed and

experienced set of conscious and unconscious experiences in which
the analyst and analysand participate. [Ogden, 1994, p. 584]

Ogden goes rather alarmingly far in his claims when he maintains that what is created by analyst and analysand is so much a
thing in itself that "there is no such thing as an analysand apart
from the relationship with the analyst". Fortunately he does not
mean it too rigorously, for he allows both parties to remember and
ponder on their own, between therapeutic encounters. More worry-
ing is the rather extreme idea that all that needs to be done, to help
at least some sufferers, is to analyse the analytic third, i.e., what
goes on between analysand and analyst when they are doing analysis. This does sound rather like maintaining that tennis is all that
matters in the life of the tennis-player and nothing affects a tennis
player's game but what happens in the game itself. Of course, that
may be true for some people, especially perhaps those who are
training to be world champions in psychoanalysis. But is it likely to
be true for the ordinary sufferer: for Mr D who has arthritis, whose
daughter refuses to sit her exams, whose lady-friend has left him,
whose holiday was rained upon every day for the third year in
succession? If we give total supremacy to those events in the intersect that are most obvious to the carefully trained analyst, we may
fall into a sad misreading of the patient's problems. However,
Ogden's practice, as we glimpse it in the illustrative case material,
is reassuring. Perhaps all we have to frown on is a style of presentation.

With Winnicott in the intersect

It was Winnicott, with his ideas on transitional space and cultural
space, who gave us non-Jungian psychotherapists in Britain
permission to look more freely at events in the intersect. He
provided a way of thinking about interpersonal experiences that
the psychoanalytic tradition had, until then, declared illusory,
sentimental, unscientific. Winnicott built on what people said about
what they felt. Tentatively, but with growing confidence, he helped
psychoanalytic psychotherapists accept their ability to, at the same
time, have and have-not, to be and not-be. Because of this, they

could start to think about experiences where the generally accepted distinction between inner and outer, self and not-self, here and not-here, might not apply with absolute strictness. He spoke and wrote bravely about:

> a part that we cannot ignore, an intermediate area of experiencing, to which inner reality and external life both contribute. [Winnicott, 1958, p. 230]

He made it possible for us to think systematically about a universe where, by virtue of a small child's creativity, a teddy-bear and a toddler could talk to each other, could support and rebuke each other, in ways quite understood by readers of A. A.Milne's Pooh stories, but about which psychotherapists had, as yet, little to say. Winnicott named this state of being an "intermediate area" of experiencing. He used the term "transitional object" for bears, comfort-blankets, and other such creations of the child's, and "transitional space" for the realm of the imagination in which such contact with bears becomes possible. At first Winnicott confined these observations to the world of babies and young children. By 1960, conveniently republished in 1965, we could be a little more confident. Winnicott was also writing about adults, and indeed about the nature of society

> In the healthy individual . . . who is a creative and spontaneous being, there is a capacity for the use of symbols . . . Health is here closely bound up with the capacity of the individual to live in an area that is intermediate between the dream and the reality, which is called the cultural life. [Winnicott, 1960, p. 150]

Of course, the toddler created the bear, but only allowed the bear autonomy in imagination. We had, after all, known since Freud that we have phantasies—the innovation was that these toddlers' phantasies were both less and more controllable than the ones we were used to noticing in our clinical work. But the concept of an *intermediate space* gave somehow permission for a way of thinking about matters more elusive and ineffable, so that we could have more precise conversations about experiences in which phenomena (not admitted to be phantasies) which were not quite one thing or another, not quite "me" and not quite "not-me", in which people may share what is "between" them, things that do not belong entirely to the one person or the other.

The concept of transitional phenomena had a very beneficial effect on psychotherapists, increasing our understanding of children's phantasy life and play, justifying an increase in the scope of playfulness in therapeutic work with both children and adults. It also had an interesting impact on English literary criticism (Bowie, 1993). For those, however, who are looking for more precise general formulations of what happens in that intermediate space, Winnicott's conceptualizations have not yet borne so much fruit, and it may be that, from the point of view of the question "What happens *between* people"?, it has been pushed as far as it can go.

Conclusion

So what do they all amount to, these affirmations and speculations by psychotherapists about intersect experiences? In my view, processes in the intersect are being variously described but, as it were, naïvely. Some central concepts needed for a coherent theory are still missing and have still to be identified and fitted into a more systematic presentation. Meanwhile, it would be worth spending a decade or so paying attention to intersect phenomena we may come across in the consulting-room and elsewhere, untidily, unpretentiously, without passionate adherence to one formulation or another, to see where it gets us in the end.

References

Allwein, G., & Barwise, J. (1996). *Logical Reasoning with Diagrams*. Oxford and New York: Oxford University Press.

Bion, W. R. (1970)[1984]. *Attention and Interpretation*. London: Karnac.

Bollas, C. (1987). *The Shadow of the Object*. London: Free Association.

Bowie, M. (1993). *Psychoanalysis and the Future of Theory*. Oxford: Blackwell Press.

Buber, M. (1923)[1937]. *I and Thou*. Edinburgh: F.T. Clark.

Eigen, M. (1998). *The Psychoanalytic Mystic*. London: Free Association.

Field, N. (1996). *Breakdown and Breakthrough*. London: Routledge.

Grotstein, Y. (1997). Bion and the pariah of 'O'. *British Journal of Psychotherapy*, 14: 77–90.

Hinshelwood, R. (1989). *A Dictionary of Kleinian Thought*. London: Free Association.

James, W. (1902). *The Varieties of Religious Experience*. London: Collins, Fontana.

Joseph, E. (1975). The patient who is difficult to reach. In: P. L. Giovacchini (Ed.), *Tactics and Techniques in Psychoanalytic Theory*. Vol. 2. New York: Jason Aronson.

Jung, C. J. (1954). *The Practice of Psychotherapy*. In: *Collected Works, 16*. London: Routledge and Kegan Paul.

Klein, J. (1995). *Doubts and Certainties in the Practice of Psychotherapy*. London: Karnac.

Ogden, T. (1979). On projective identification. *International Journal of Psychoanalysis*, 60: 357–373.

Ogden, T. (1982). *Projective Identification and Psychotherapeutic Technique*. New York: Jason Aronson.

Ogden, T. (1994). The analytic third: working with intersubjective clinical facts. *International Journal of Psychoanalysis*, 75: 883–900.

Redfearn, J. (1985). *Myself, My Many Selves*. Vol. 6. London: Library of Analytic Psychology.

Searles, H. (1960). *The Non-Human Environment in Normal Development and in Schizophrenia*. New York: International Universities Press.

Searles, H. (1979). *Countertransference and Related Subjects*. New York: International Universities Press.

Williams, C. (1931)[1952]. *Many Dimensions*. Harmondsworth: Penguin.

Williams, C. (1933). *The Place of the Lion*. Re-issued Grand Rapids, USA: William B. Eerdmans Publishing Co.

Williams, C. (1937). *Descent into Hell*. London: Longman Green.

Winnicott, D. W. (1958). *Collected papers: Through Paediatrics to Psychoanalysis*. London: Hogarth Press.

Winnicott, D. W. (1971). *Playing and Reality*. London: Tavistock Publications [reprinted London: Penguin, 1974].

Wright, K. (1996). Looking after the self. In: V. Richards (Ed.) *The Person Who is Me*. London: Karnac.

Zaehner, R. C. (1957). *Mysticism, Sacred and Profane*. Oxford: University Press.

RESPONSE BY PATRICK CASEMENT

There is so much richness in Jo Klein's paper that I think my best course is to pick out just some of the gems that I most valued, while also offering some of my own thoughts on her topic.

The ineffable

There is a striking paradox here as we attempt to address the ineffable: that which is "too great to be expressed in words" (*New Oxford Dictionary*). What we are able to conceive of, as we attempt to address the ineffable, can only be the merest shadow of what it is that lies beyond what we are trying to address. And, in relation to those we meet with, there is the "not I" in each other person that lies beyond anything that we can hope to know, if we seek to know it only through that process of "recognizing ourselves in others" that Searles speaks of.

It is, of course, a fundamental part of trying to tune into another person that we aim to put ourselves empathically into their shoes, in the context of their life story, with their particular experiences and sensitivities, in order to imagine how this person might see life and feel about its many vicissitudes. But, in our clinical work, this trial-identifying with the patient can only take us so far. What is most uniquely true of the other person will always lie beyond our own imagining.

So, we are likely to recognize the familiar in the other much more readily than that which is unfamiliar. In this regard, our understanding of the other will always be limited, particularly when we prefer to remain on well- trodden ground, mapped out for us by our theories, rather than being faced by that which can be disorientating, even at times dread-full, about another person's perception of life, in all its unfamiliarity and strangeness. It is in the unfamiliarity of the "other" that we are most challenged. And sometimes we will defend ourselves against the unfamiliar in our patients, for there we are most likely to find ourselves feeling incompetent and out of our depth. Facing the unknown will always be a far greater challenge than staying with the known.

It is here that we are most likely to be confronted by the ineffable. And that is why I take issue with Searles. I think Searles is right as far as he goes, in advocating that we must be able to recognize ourselves in others. Not only does this give us a way into understanding the other, it also helps to prevent us falling into the "I–it" relating that Buber warns us against. Jo Klein rightly comments: "The only changes in an I–it encounter—if encounter it can be called—happens in the head of the person who is talking . . .".

And this "I–it" relating is what can happen, even without our noticing it, when we begin to see a patient as the object of our psychological study. We can then sit back, imagining that we are in the presence of someone not like us. And that is why it is certainly useful also to be reminded by Searles that the more we know ourselves, the more we are able to recognize ourselves in others. But this is where I think we need to go beyond what Searles is advocating. For, if we see only ourselves, or primarily ourselves, in the other, we will limit our awareness of the otherness of the other.

By seeing ourselves in the other I am not just thinking of direct similarities we might find between a patient and ourselves. I am including here our clinical experience also, in that we can so easily get into generalizing from other clinical experience. Here we can fall into the illusion that our work with another patient, who has had similar experiences, might offer us a shortcut to understanding the patient who is now with us. I think that almost any linking we make between similar patients is likely to lead us into relating to the familiar more readily than to recognizing that which is different.

I agree with Nathan Field that "the surgical probe of insight cannot melt the frozen core" that we encounter in some of our patients. Much more is needed if we are to meet these patients where they most need to be met. We need to be able to be alongside a patient, in an "I–Thou" relationship, not sitting back in detachment from a patient's inner life and pain. So, when we are dealing with something difficult for a patient, we, too, will find it difficult. If we imagine that we can deal with it easily, we only show how little we are in touch with the patient's difficulty.

If we are really to deal with a patient's pain, we also will be in pain. I take this to be a *sine qua non* in analytic work, if it is to be therapeutic as well as analytic. So, if we remain detached from a patient's pain I think we must realize that we are defending ourselves and, to that extent, we will not be able to change much for the patient. It will be clear by now that I am not only considering the ineffable as referring to that which lies beyond normal experience, and may well lie beyond our own experience. I am including that which lies beyond our awareness of the otherness of the other.

Jo Klein gives us some special gems when she illustrates Grotstein and Eigen ". . . writing with respect about phenomena shunned by more pin-striped psychoanalysts". And what a gem she also finds in Buber, in his description of an infant's wonderment at the world around, as the infant's eyes and hands "settle on the red carpet-pattern . . . not [to] be moved until the soul of the red has opened itself to them". Would that we could retain more of that wonderment as, it is to be hoped, we lay ourselves open to the otherness of the other that we can meet in our patients.

Jo Klein pointedly reminds us that the dreadful as well as the sublime may be encountered through ineffable experience. She recalls that Winnicott had the inspiration to recognize that huge anxieties about future breakdown arise from repressed memories of an unbearable event that has already happened. So it may be that the overwhelming power of ineffable experience, in all that is most sublime and all that is most to be dreaded, stems from experiences we have already had, however much they may have been idealized or demonized by our own minds.

Or might there be a dimension in life that some people experience, but which others seem not to have experienced? Or a few people may have experienced in part while not daring to recognize what could lie beyond their own comprehension. So, we need to wonder: how do people relate to such experiences in others if they themselves have never experienced anything similar? Who are we to know the truth of another's experience? Are we right to limit our perspective only to that to which we ourselves are prepared to give credence? What if there is more in life than we are open to, but to which others may be open? What then?

Carrying another's pain?

I now wish to dwell a while on the marvellous extract that Jo Klein quotes from Charles Williams. I think that this gives us a useful start in thinking about how we might begin to help bear the burden of another. But, however compelling the vision may be that is offered by Williams, I regard this as having serious shortcomings which I now wish to address.

Williams is, of course, not a therapist. Instead, he offers his own charismatic view of being the kind of helper he wished to imagine he could be. I shall quote only the opening lines of those given by Jo Klein. The person in distress says: "How can anyone else carry your fear? Can anyone else see it and have to meet it?" To this comes the reply: "Has no one ever relieved you of that? Haven't you ever asked them to? . . . And if not, will you let me do it for you? . . . Then you needn't fear it . . ." And promises: "I will give myself to it, and imagine it, and know it. And then you won't."

My problem with this, as a psychoanalyst/therapist, is that Williams here is presenting the seduction of omnipotence. This allows him to believe that he can magic away the fear of another person. Also, he makes it sound so easy. But that is the essence of magic. And he adds this point in his own way: "And what can be easier than for me to carry for a little while a burden that isn't mine?"

But if we consider the task of the therapist, when confronted by the fear or the pain of another, I believe that there is no way that we can take this from them. At most we may be able to enter into it—alongside the patient—as far as we are able, knowing that even then the patient's fear and pain will essentially remain beyond our own imagining. We can only get near to it, knowing that we cannot entirely know how it really is for the other person.

I think that we also need to bear in mind that we cannot do what the other person may be asking of us, or that we may most want to do for them—as Charles Williams also wished. We cannot remove the pain. We cannot remove the fear. At most we can try to see that the other person is not so alone with it as before. That may be the only thing we can offer. And we cannot know that it will actually make any difference: only that it just *might* make a difference. I regard this as the potency of shared helplessness, which does not mean that we are necessarily as helpless as the patient feels. We hope to be able to bear being in touch with the unbearable. This includes being in touch with the despair, willing at least to stay with it for however long—not knowing that it will help.

What we can be sure of, however, is that it could be even worse for the patient if we, too, could not bear to be in touch with what others before seem to have been unable to bear. If there is eventually to be any relief for the patient I believe it lies in our willingness to be in touch with their experience. It is not in carrying hope for the patient but in entering into the patient's despair and being willing to bear it alongside the patient.

If we seek to reassure the patient by suggesting that we are carrying hope for them (which we may also do—but silently) the patient is likely to hear this (unconsciously) as evidence that we are not willing, or are not able, to be any more than slightly in touch with their own deepest dread. But if we are more fully in touch with that dread we may also be feeling something of the patient's own hopelessness, too. I think that we have to find in ourselves, if we can, a capacity to be in both places simultaneously: entering into the patient's hopelessness so that we feel it too, and yet not destroyed by it.

This is how I think we can engage, as therapists, with the intersect that Jo Klein speaks of: remaining within the intersect, feeling as fully as may be what the patient is feeling; and at the same time, in the non-intersect, still being able to hold on to our own sanity and our capacity to go on, despite the fear and the dread that we are feeling alongside the patient.

References

See Josephine Klein's paper.

What is religion?

Karen Armstrong

(This paper has been transcribed from the original tape recording and edited with the author's approval.)

When I have previously discussed the links between psychotherapy and spirituality, I have usually concentrated on mysticism, which I regard as a discipline that descends into the depths of the psyche where one discovers a centre of meaning. I think, perhaps, that psychotherapy is a secular form of mysticism where, with the aid of a therapist, you go step by step down into the depths of the self in search of meaning.

But on this occasion I wish to consider the topic of religion generally, because mysticism, like psychotherapy, is only for a small minority. Only a limited number of people can afford psychotherapy, and very few, however religious they are, have the ability to be a mystic. I have tried for years and have been completely unable to do so. It is a talent, like being able to play the piano. You can take a few lessons but you soon discover whether you are a virtuoso or not. In the larger perspective, mysticism is a small though important religious enthusiasm.

Instead I want to consider why people have been religious and are continuing to be religious up to the present day. As soon as our apeman ancestors came down from the trees and became recognizably human, they began to create works of art and evolve religions. It continued in this way for millennia, but in the secular Western world by the middle of the last century, it seemed inevitable that religion would gradually wither away. Yet worldwide there has been a rebellion against secularism; not so much here in the UK, but throughout much of the world, and certainly in the United States. Why has there been this unforeseen religious revival? Why is *homo sapiens* essentially *homo religiosus*?

First, because we are meaning-seeking creatures. I suspect that many of the people who seek out a psychotherapist are in search of some kind of meaning in a life that constantly seems arbitrary, bizarre, cruel, frightening, and disturbing. Human beings find it almost impossible to exist except in a context of meaning. That doesn't mean always finding answers but it means that as one listens to a great piece of music, or to a great work of literature, one has a sense that there is a grounding of meaning and significance. Second, we seek meaning because human beings appear to be the only animals who have to live with the knowledge of their own mortality. It is a factor unique to the human condition, and something we always find difficult. Dogs, as far as we know, don't spend a great deal of time agonizing about the canine condition or about the plight of dogs in various parts of the world. We do. This is part of our human nature. It is both our curse and our great gift; a prime source of human creativity.

From Freud onwards psychotherapy aspired to be seen as a science, and still does. I always think it closer to an art form myself, just as religion is an art form. The great mistake has been to imagine that religious doctrines are statements of objective fact. That is a huge inaccuracy, but it is one that a lot of people fall into. There is a lot of bad religion around—not least among some of our religious leaders—just as there is a lot of bad psychotherapy around, too.

Perhaps because we are meaning-seeking creatures, we are also creatures that fall very easily into despair. And that is why people seek therapy, and it is why for centuries people have turned to religion. It is to work out some sense that, despite all the dispiriting

and depressing evidence to the contrary, life does have some ultimate meaning or value, even if you can't articulate clearly what that
is. As human beings we are not only appalled by the suffering that
we see all around us, the pain, the injustice, the natural disasters,
we are also struck with wonder at the universe. We are creatures
that seek ecstasy. That doesn't necessarily mean that we want to
freak out into alternative states of consciousness, but we seek out
those experiences where we are touched deeply within, momentar-
ily beyond ourselves. Ecstasy meant originally to "stand outside"
the self, where for a time we leave the limitations of ourselves
behind. We get that in art too. Music gives one a sense of transcendence, a resonance within one's own being; we find it in painting,
in literature, and, for a great many people, even sport—especially if
we don't find it in religion.

In the pre-modern world, because art was mostly confined to
rich men's homes, religion was, for many, the chief source of ecstasy.
It was religion that gave the kind of structures, especially when
associated with art, that provided a sense of transcendence. One
of the peculiarities of the human mind is that we are able to have
experiences and ideas that transcend. We seek these things out. And
if we don't find ecstasy in one outlet, we will look for it in another.
People in this country are no longer finding it in the churches, so
they are voting with their feet and leaving. In the UK only about
six per cent of the population attend a religious service regularly,
as opposed to nearly seventy per cent in the United States.

Now, faith is not about believing things. This is one of the major
mistakes we have made in recent years. The last time I made this
statement in public someone called out, "Well, what is faith then?"
Let me repeat: faith is not belief. If you look at the scriptures of all
the major religions, if you read, for example, what Jesus actually
said, hardly a single doctrine passes his lips. There is no talk about
Trinity or Incarnation or Original Sin or Atonement, all of which are
regarded as crucially important to Christianity. He is talking
primarily about the importance of reaching out and being kind.

The Buddha had huge impatience with metaphysical thinking.
He was bored by it. Because he knew it wouldn't help. The Buddha
was once pestered by a monk who kept asking: "Is there a god or
not? Who created the world? Was the world created in time or is it
eternal." Finally the Buddha told him he was like a man who had

been shot with a poisonous arrow but who refused to have any medical treatment until he had found out the name of his assailant and what village he came from. He said, "You will die before you get this perfectly pointless information." The Koran, too, is highly sceptical about metaphysical speculation. It calls it *vana*: self-indulgent guesswork. And the Koran is constantly astonished that people quarrel about matters that nobody can prove one way or the other, creating huge bitterness, if not murderousness, between people who should be united.

When you say you have faith in a person, or an idea, or in some ultimate meaning, it has to be cultivated. You reach it not by accepting a metaphysical doctrine and then putting it into practice. That's how science works: first you establish a theory, then you apply it and test it by experiment. But in the religious world, as in the world of art, that is not how it works. When you want to expose yourself to music, you don't sit down first and work out the theory of tonality. You come to music by listening and training your ear. People expect religion to be instantly apprehensible but that is as inane as to go into an art gallery without having seen a single example of Western art. We have to train our religious sense, cultivate it consciously by doing some quite hard work. But it is not belief.

The word "credo" in Latin comes from *cordero*—to give your heart. You give your heart to this and then you will understand. You live in a certain way and you acquire a different perspective. Religion requires contemplation, it requires the cultivation of particular cast of mind. It is an ethical aesthetic. The Buddha said, "Once you live in a certain way and make that habitual, then you will know what Nirvana is". When asked if Nirvana exists, he would say, "It is an improper question. There are no words or concepts that provide a valid answer."

I now realize that this is what has happened to me. Throughout my childhood and youth I had bad religious experience. So for years I wanted nothing to do with religion. But years of studying it in a certain way have brought a change. And when people ask me "Well, do you or do you not believe in a God?" the question fills me with sudden weariness. I can see it is inept because that is just not what it is about. It's more a transformation of consciousness that takes place gradually over time and makes you see things in a different way.

In the pre-modern world, it was taken for granted that human beings had two main ways of approaching truth. One the Greeks called *mythos*, myth; the other *logos*, meaning reason. We have always needed science, logic, reason, to run our societies efficiently. We need technology, even to get an arrow to hit its target. Logos is part of our life. But we also need myth, which is never intended to be taken as literal fact. Both of these were complementary, neither was superior to the other, and it was very dangerous for one to encroach on the other. If you used myth to run your daily affairs or your political life, you were in for a disaster. The Crusades were an example of *mythos* used in entirely the wrong way.

By the same token, reason can't answer our human perplexities. If your child dies you don't want a reasoned discourse on why this has happened. You want to sit in silence, or listen to a piece of music, or take part in a religious rite. Myths have to be activated by ritual. Psychotherapy has recourse to all kinds of myths: the Oedipus myth, the myth of Narcissus, and many more. They all encompass deep psychological truths. But they need to be activated by ritual, and certain rituals that may seem arcane and absurd to an outsider are enacted in the consulting room. There is the pretence that there is no one else in the house. No one must be heard coming in and going out. In therapy, time is kept with an almost religious intensity. These strict boundaries are a way of creating a type of art form; something approaching a mystery, which happens in a different dimension. The ritual lifts them off the page and makes them work.

Unless a historical fact is mythologized it cannot become a religious idea. A typical example is the well known Biblical myth of the Exodus from Egypt of the ancient Israelites. In our scientific age, well-meaning people have tried to prove that, thanks to the prevalence of flash flooding in the region, Pharaoh's army all drowned. This is quite beside the point, because the story is written precisely as a myth; the mythology of the East was continually talking about God creating new entities by splitting the sea in half. It also refers to the rite of passage whereby you go through water and come out changed. The Exodus myth is re-activated by the Jews every year by the ritual of the Passover meal. It has been transformed from a bizarre event in history to something that has resonated for millennia in the life of the Jewish people. It was St Paul who made the historical Jesus into a myth and therefore transformed Christianity into a viable religion. Muslims have done the same with Muhammad by means of their art and by their Islamic law, which lifts the prophet from the confines of the seventh century and makes him into a living reality in the heart of present-day Islamic life.

From about the eighteenth century logos began to achieve such spectacular results that myth became discredited. Nowadays, in popular parlance, myth simply means something that's not true. When asked about the peccadillos of his private life a politician will say, "It's a myth, it didn't happen." If you had asked the ancient Greeks taking part in the Eleusian mysteries whether Persephone had really descended into the underworld, they would have looked at you as though you were an idiot, because the myth is expressing something deeper, something that cannot always be put into clear logical propositions. Other people's myths, like the myths of psychotherapy, often sound absurd to an outsider, but they work in the context of your commitment to them. That is what religion does. If you seek to turn your myth into logos you are creating both bad religion and bad science, because the two are complementary.

The West has long been quite a bit better at logos than myth. You can see it very clearly in the division between the Greek Orthodox Churches and the Western Churches. There was a schism between them which was triggered by the politics of the eleventh century. But the underlying split came from the fact that the Greeks and Latins were each developing quite different ideas about God and the divine. The Greeks thought that the Latins were developing too rationalistic an idea of God: that God's existence could be proved or spoken about in the terms of logos.

Let me offer two telling examples. In Greece you can't study theology, which is the study of God, unless you are engaged in theoria, which means contemplation. You cannot be a theologian unless you are taking part in ritual and prayer. From the Greek perspective it is like trying to be a skater without ever setting foot on the ice.

The other example derives from the word dogma. Greeks always separated the two parts of religion into corigma and dogma. Corigma was that part of Christianity that can be explained to outsiders. "Well there was this man Jesus of Nazareth and he died and we believe he rose from the dead and was divine." Dogma on the other hand is everything in religion that cannot be imparted in that clear way but something that you learn slowly, which you acquire, as you acquire fondness for a person. It is done by means of the practice: contemplation and liturgy and your ethical conduct. Now we in the West have made dogma into the exact opposite. It is everything that we can articulate, so that we can make sure everybody else believes with us.

The Buddha would have said it was the most "unskilful" idea. He liked to tell the story of a traveller who came to a great expanse of water and desperately needed to get across. But there was no bridge and no ferry. So he cobbled together a raft and paddled it across. "But then," the Buddha asked his monks "what is he supposed to do with the raft now? Is he supposed to say, 'This raft has saved my life, therefore I must put it on my back and lug it around for the rest of my days'? Or does he simply mourn the raft and go on his journey? The answer is obvious. Remember that my teachings are like that raft. If they get you across the river of pain, fine, but don't make a millstone of them." The Buddha would have been impatient with those Christians who are still endlessly tinkering with doctrines that made sense in the fourth century in order to make them acceptable in the twentieth century. For many devout Christians, these are difficult ideas.

So, religion, what is it? Many things, but first: religion begins in an experience of suffering. All the great religions put the fact of suffering absolutely at the forefront of their concern. Later generations came to equate suffering with lack of faith. If you are suffering, or perplexed, or confused, or distressed, this is incompatible with faith, which should give you iron hard certainty. A convinced Christian once said to me, "With faith, I never have a moment's doubt, never a moment's suffering or distress." We were in Cheltenham at the time. I thought that perhaps if he was living in a part of the world where you can't get away from suffering, he might have more difficulty. I asked how he felt about the concentration camps? He seemed to think that a concentration camp would be a breeze to a man with faith.

Not one of the great founders of the world religions—Buddha, Jesus, the Hebrew prophets, or Muhammad—would have had any truck with such an attitude. Socrates, another of the great figures of the Axial Age, says that the philosophical quest cannot begin until you lose your certainty, until the things that you take for granted you suddenly feel doubt about. To be confused is the beginning of wisdom. To try to block out suffering is a denial of the spiritual quest. I'm sure the same process applies in the therapist's consulting room: if a client resolutely denies their suffering they will get nowhere. Only when they realize their pain, and recognize the pain of others, can things begin to change.

How can we reach this frame of mind? There is a special attitude that I have found in all the world's great religions that I will call, for want of a better word, by its Greek term *kenosis*, self-emptying. The first thing the prophet Muhammad did when he began to preach in Mecca was not to accept any doctrines. He used to make his listeners prostate themselves three times a day in prayer facing the direction of Jerusalem. This was hard for Bedouins who found it demeaning to grovel on the ground like slaves. But the attitude of the body in that characteristic posture of Muslim prayer instructed the mind at a level deeper than rational thought. A true Muslim is a man or a woman who has surrendered their whole being to the demands of the divine. That is symbolized in the posture of *salat*, the Muslim prayer which is meant to be an educative exercise. Often the body teaches us things better than just cerebral discourse. Until you have given up this feeling of *istaka* (self-sufficiency) and surrendered yourself to your suffering, to your fear, to your confusions, until you can give up your greed and selfishness, then you can't begin to claim that you have faith.

One of the earliest New Testament texts is Second Phillippians, which talks about "the Word of God emptying itself". God emptied himself when he took the form on earth of a criminal blasphemer and finally accepted the disgraceful death of crucifixion. In our personal life, when we wake up at three a.m. and toss and turn in our unhappiness, it is very often because of the "me"—because I am not appreciated, because I haven't got this, that, or the other, because I am "full of myself", not "empty of myself".

There is a sixteenth century Jewish cabbalistic myth that speaks of God limiting himself. It was enunciated by the great rabbi and mystic Isaac Luria, after the Jews were expelled from Spain, which they regarded as a catastrophe. It first took root among these exiles from Spain, but became (and this is the important point) a mass movement throughout the Jewish world. What Luria did was to rewrite the Biblical myth of creation. Instead of the Genesis story, where God created the world in seven days and blessed it, where everything was peaceful and under God's control, Luria's myth reflects the violence of the world that he was living in and the catastrophe his fellow Jews had experienced. Luria presented creation as a series of terrible explosions, a succession of false starts where God had to try and try again!

Nobody among the devout Jews protested that this was not in the Bible, that you can't just change a creation myth like that. They knew that myths are all ways of responding to difficult questions. The difficult, essential question is: how can there be something rather than nothing? Luria's answer became a mass movement right across the Jewish world. It begins with God making an act of violence against Himself. It says, mythically speaking, if God is everywhere, there is no place for anything else but God. So, in order to bring something else into being, God evacuated a region within Himself to make room for the world. Creation thus begins with an act of self-diminishment. The Hebrew word is *tsimtsum* (withdrawal). It was as if God was withdrawing voluntarily, to bring something new, something other than Himself, into being.

The Muslims also have a myth with a similar theme: before creation God said, as it were: "I am the hidden treasure that yearns to be known". He felt huge sorrow for all the beings that didn't exist and would therefore never know him. So he gave a great sigh of compassion from the depths of his being and in that sigh, created the world. These myths arise because people find that this is what life is like. They don't just happen because they edify, but because they work.

What God did is the example for mankind to follow. That is, when you give up a part of yourself, when you come out of your self-sufficiency, when you empty yourself, and when, above all, you are motivated by compassion, that is the ethical imperative of religion.

When I talk about *kenosis* or giving up self, etc., I do not mean that kind of awful spirituality that I was subjected to where you are endlessly bashing yourself and telling yourself how terrible you are and doing ridiculous penances. I spent years in my convent doing just this, crawling round on the ground and kissing people's feet— and it is a complete waste of time. None of the leaders of the great world religions go in for this kind of nonsense. It is just another form of narcissism that embeds you in the very self you are trying to transcend. What I am talking about is not a bright little idea of my own but what I have found in my studies of the great world traditions. The way to make your myth into a vibrant reality in your life is by compassion. The Dalai Llama was asked recently what his religion is about and he simply said: it is about being kind. Jesus consistently emphasized compassion, but he was an excitable type and sometimes he seems to have fallen, as we all do, from his high ideals. The bedrock message of the Koran is that you must create a just and peaceful society where poor and vulnerable people are treated the same as the rich and powerful. If you live in that way you will know God and your society will prosper. If you don't, you won't. So compassion is the key and I think the religions have lost this. They have concentrated on being "right" and a lot of people prefer to be right than to be kind.

The great Rabbi Hillel, a contemporary of Jesus, was once asked to sum up the whole of Jewish teaching, the Torah, while he stood on one leg. A group of Gentiles came to him and said, "If you can do that, we'll convert to Judaism." Hillel stood on one leg and said, "Do not do unto others as you would not have done unto you. That is the Torah. The rest is commentary. Go and learn it."

Now that is an extraordinary statement. There is nothing about the Nature of God, the Holy Land, the revelation of the Torah on Mount Sinai. If we really lived like that—if every time we were tempted to say something unkind or untrue about another person we stopped to ask ourselves: "How would I like that said about me?"—in that moment one will have transcended one's self. And that is what religion is.

Five hundred years or so before Hillel, Confucius had come out with exactly the same notion: do not do unto others as you would not have done unto you. Jesus taught an active version of that golden rule: "do unto others as you would have done unto you". I teach in a college and my students and I have many happy hours wrangling about which is the more stringent requirement: doing or refraining from doing? The Great Rabbi (Joshua Heschel) used to say that if we put ourselves at the opposite pole of ego, we are in the place where God is. I can have faith that moves mountains, but if I lack charity it is worth nothing.

I lived for years in extremely unkind communities in a convent, and then at Oxford. Everyone was always blasting off against other people for the highest possible reasons and there was no way you could have proper religious experiences in those circumstances, because you become like it yourself. The only way in which to survive in that world is to learn to sit back. Over the years I have had to work very hard at myself to do this because I have this sharp tongue, and I learned at my reverend mother's knee to give as good as I got. I also know that since I have been involved in this quest (from morning to night in the study of religion, which is my form of prayer) I have found myself incapable of enduring unkindness whether it is to myself or to others. It is a social liability, because I become utterly depressed. It is very hard to bear, but that is what religion should do to you. It is somehow what it has done to me.

Religion in this century has lost the plot, as we saw in the 11 September outrage. Fundamentalism has erupted in every single major world religion, often characterized by rage and anger. That is because the fundamentalists feel profoundly threatened and that is where hatred kicks in.

As soon as you speak unkindly of another human being, let alone kill another person, you have, in religious terms, lost the plot. Sometimes religious people look furious when this is brought up, because it is no fun being religious if you can't disapprove of other people. I think we must also include the secular fundamentalists, who take as hostile a view of religion as the religious fundamentalists do of secularism. This is the mean part of humanity that perverts the ethic of compassion at the heart of all world religions. We should feel, whatever ideology we subscribe to, respect for the sacredness that inhabits every single human being and, indeed, our environment.

INDEX